Feline Humans

Feline Humans

A Timeless Exchange
of
Love and Light

Material channeled from
Arvantis of the Arkoreuns
by SHAUN SWANSON

Questions developed and asked
by JEFFERSON VISCARDI

Published by: Sounds of Light Communications

www.Arvantis.org

ISBN 978-0-9844108-1-1

First Edition, December 2010

Printed in the United States of America

Acknowledgments

We express brilliant rainbows of gratitude to Arvantis and the Arkoreuns for their sharing and support in the inspired co-creation of this book! It is the second book in our "Galactic Family Series."

Warm waves of love to everyone around the world for your direct and indirect support in strengthening the positive relationships that are being established with our galactic family. It's wonderful to have so many people on Earth realizing the rich support our extra-terrestrial relatives can give us as we welcome the vast knowledge and expansive life experiences they share with us.

Jefferson extends a lovely word of appreciation to his heroes: young master Jesus for his most enlightening life teachings and examples of unconditional love, the writer and Italian philosopher Giordano Bruno for his inspirational endurance and perseverance, and J also thanks his mom, Eva Batista dos Santos, dad, Jair Viscardi and his older brother Wagner Batista Viscardi.

Shaun thanks Arvantis, the Arkoreuns, Gilgamesh and also the Group of Friends for their intriguing inspiration and their powerfully loving support during the adventurous development of this book! Shaun also sends a warm hug of gratitude to:
Alex Cross, Clare Patterson, Daniel Bronk, Darryl Anka, David Bartholomew, David Thomas, Drunvalo, Frank Viauso, Florence Riggs, Glen Tobias, Ione Linker, Kam Yuen, Ken Klingbeil, Kevin Ryerson, Krista Kirkwood, Lee Carroll, Liah Howard, Linda Tesar, Margaret Rogers, Phil Angemaier, Sharon Marvel, Shawn Randall, Sheridan Hailley, Sonya Fairbanks, Uri Geller, Violet Schindler, and Gene and Barbara Swanson.

Preface

Arvantis is a human Extra-Terrestrial and Jefferson Viscardi is a human Terrestrial. The wealth of information that's contained in this book is the result of their ET & T conversations together.

The conversations that were recorded for this book took place between October 19th, 2009 and April 10th, 2010. During each of the conversations, Jefferson Viscardi was in Belmont, California, and Shaun Swanson, who channeled Arvantis, was on the Island of Maui in Hawaii.

Although some editing was done to account for the language differences, the majority of the material in this book was transcribed verbatim from the audio recordings.

This book is the second in our "Galactic Family Series." The first book is "Avatars of the Phoenix Lights UFO: Ishuwa and the Yahyel."

For more information on Arvantis and other highly loving and intelligent ETs or Star Beings in our genetically related Galactic Family, visit the following sites:

www.arvantis.org
and www. youtube.com/user/felinehumanoid

www.ishuwa.com
and www. youtube.com/user/ishuwadotcom

www.yahyel.com
and www. youtube.com/user/theyahyel

The Four Laws of Creation

One:

You Exist.

The way that you exist can change, but you always exist in some way, shape, or form.

(State of being: Oneness and beingness.)

Two:

The One is the All, and the All are the One.

(State of being: Connection and separation.)

Three:

What you put out is what you get back.

Also known as the "Law of Attraction."

(State of being: Reflection and attraction.)

Four:

Change is the only constant, except the first three laws which never change.

Everything changes except the first three laws.

(State of being: Experiences you have as a result of actions you take.)

Table of Contents

- Our genetic connection with your world.
- Information about our solar system.
- Appearance of our planet's surface.
- Night vision built-in to our biology.
- Food on our world.
- Modes of travel.
- House designs that we have on our planet.
- Arvantis has a brother and sisters too.
- Memories of Arkoreun childhood.
- Arkoreun chant.
- Arvantis unveils how he discovered Jefferson on Earth.
- The first communications between Arvantis and Jefferson.
- Jefferson attends a group event on the Arkoreun's planet.
- Steps that can facilitate contact with human ETs.
- Where our names come from.
- Aging with joy and without illness.
- Some characteristics of our ET body.
- What our culture values in life.

Chapter 2
Uncovering the Real World of Human ETs
page 31

- Arvantis describes the studio he transmits his live messages from.
- How his live messages to us are received.
- Orbs we send to you.
- Yahyel and Arkoreun visitations, a gathering of human ETs.
- Soul sharing through time and space.
- Arvantis talks about talking with Giordano Bruno (1548–1600).
- Details of Giordano's life and personal growth.
- How Arkoreuns experience **time** in their lives.
- Weather on planet Revision 5, in the OrOctal Solar System.
- Fashionable clothing options.
- Teeth and Tongue for diet and digestion.
- Intelligent Life on two other planets in our 14-planet solar system.
- Self-governing churchless civilizations living joyfully.
- Arkoreun chakra system and function.
- Feline Men and Women dating and in love.

Chapter 3
Extraterrestrial Dragons and Earth Spacecrafts
page 61

- Jefferson's contact with a Zeta from Earth's parallel reality.
- Arvantis visits with Jefferson on Earth.
- Purpose of Arvantis's visit.
- Orbits around Suns, and living without annual calendars.
- Spacecrafts that your world will design are on the horizon.
- Jefferson visits 4 other planets.
- Arkoreun spacecrafts and their space pilots.
- Ages of Arvantis's brother and sisters.
- Animals on the Arkoreun's planet.
- Visitations by intelligent extraterrestrial dragons.
- Interplanetary communications in the OrOctal Solar System.
- Appreciating others by having festive celebrations in nature.
- Arvantis's brother, Orse, asks Jefferson about *fixture replacements*.

Chapter 4
Excellent Extraterrestrial Experiences, EEE

- Arvantis - Biological Scientist of living organisms.
- The first in-person contact between Arvantis and Jefferson.
- Bridging the language gap by using an inner Universal language.
- Types of arrangements that are made before contact is made.
- Arkoreun fashions of organic attire.
- Detailed insights on Arkoreun eyesight.
- Jefferson's growth in life awareness due to human-ET encounters.
- The role that human's collective consciousness plays in Contact.
- Activating codes in DNA to access expansive knowledge of life.
- Postcard deliveries from other planets.
- Could an Earth human live on planet Revision 5?
- Arvantis describes interacting with Frupees - Koala Bears.

Chapter 5
Rewriting the "Wrongs"

- Spell our civilization's name in the way that works best for you.
- Arvantis goes on a streamside walk at sunset with the local wildlife.
- The color purple that flows within us.
- A planet undergoing atmospheric and geological regeneration.
- A Zeta human-ET makes new choices that will rewrite the 'wrongs'.
- Progress made on interplanetary postcard delivery.
- Arkoreuns have all they need to joyfully thrive on planet Revision 5.
- What life on Earth might be like 357 years in the future.
- How "windows for contact" come into being.
- Arvantis meets with Jefferson's Zeta guide to facilitate new contacts.
- Estimate for time of physical ET contact in public.
- Jefferson's move from San Francisco, California, to São Paulo, Brazil.
- Clues to help Jefferson find out what *replacing fixtures* is all about.

Chapter 6
Soul Mates, Twin Flames & One Night Stands

- Communicating with soul reflections on other timelines.
- Can a Feline human from Revision 5 live on Earth?
- Daily diets.
- Arvantis met Bashar, a human ET from Essassani, on a spaceship.
- Words from our heart work better for us than flowers for the girl.
- Soul Mates, Twin Flames & one-night stands in heartfelt intimacy.
- The Arkoreun tongue, heart, hand, feet, whiskers, nose & head.
- Different digestion systems & internal organs inside Feline humans.
- Arkoreuns don't pray to an external god.
- K-PAX, Arvantis, Jefferson, walk-ins and walk-outs.

Chapter 7
How To Be of Greatest Service To Others

- You are of greatest service to others when you follow your heart.
- Designing physical life forms to fit in with their physical world.
- Feline eyes, lips, and belly buttons.
- Seven to eleven months in our mother's womb.
- Home grown clothing.
- Arvantis visits Earth before and after the current human era.
- Let go of focusing on facts that fog your vision of reality.
- Accessing a parallel past to increase ones knowledge today.
- Jefferson's after-death experience from a previous lifetime.
- Going-away celebrations for those with pre-set life departure dates.
- Jefferson coexists on a planet in Andromeda.
- Organic houses, rivers and rainfall.
- Time travel to Earth in 2012.

Chapter 8
Living Harmoniously in Your True Design

- How can a week go by with no passage of time?
- There's nothing missing in life when you actually follow your heart.
- Sacred Geometry as a tool to remember your oneness with all life.
- Giordano breaks free from life's illusory prison, while he's in jail.
- Jefferson's past life incarnation meets Jesus for the first time.
- Shaun's past life incarnation meets Jefferson's past life incarnation.
- Unmentioned Apostles of Jesus.
- Your heart's internal guidance will support you in life 100%.
- Disruptive beliefs within the collective consciousness.
- How to live in your highest excitement.
- Equality of beliefs.
- Appreciation and support from Arvantis's planet.
- It's all beautiful, all the time, 24/7.
- These transactions facilitate the manifesting of the day we will meet.

Chapter 9
The Prime Creator Is All of Us

- Jefferson's treasures of wisdom for Arvantis.
- Creating the illusion of past, present, and future can be fun.
- You create the idea of "this moment" and "here and now."
- I am, therefore I can think.
- Definition of the prime Creator from Arvantis the Arkoreun.
- Existence does not have a built-in meaning.
- The Four Laws of Creation.
- Tune in to your hearts emotions for optimal physical vitality.
- All That Is.
- Translating an Arkoreun phrase into English.
- 3 societies of ETs that have human genes are here with us today.
- A spacecraft several miles in size with only 15,000 ETs aboard.

Chapter 10
Entering the 5th Dimension of Heart Vibrations

- Jefferson has more than nine lives in parallel realities.
- Born in a group of extraterrestrials.
- Arkoreuns are vastly different from the Na'vi in the Avatar film.
- Earth humans are entering the 5th dimension of heart vibrations.
- The old and limiting belief systems on Earth are being dismantled.
- The Rorkin ETs harvesting a food that activates higher awareness.
- Jefferson's pre-birth visit to the Arcturus region of space.
- The moon is to tides as ETs can be to our biology & awareness.
- Postcards and Amulets.
- Luminary light at night without bulbs and wires of electric life.
- There are foods that can support attainment of self-realization.
- Rescinding laws that make it illegal to have contact with ET life.

Chapter 11
Smiling in the Mirror of Physical Reality

- Shadow governments and our "play of limitation and darkness."
- Hiding your true heart due to fear of an external god.
- As more of you follow your heart, secret governments fall away.
- Escape the prison cell of illusory beliefs and become heavenly free.
- Following your heart creates financial support when you believe it.
- Engaging in these excellent attitudes activates Creator awareness.
- The evaporation of sinners, declining bank accounts, and militaries.
- Your infrastructures are ascending through heart centered people.
- Fear of ETs vanishes when you let go of alien beliefs about life.
- Everything is possible, recognize what is probable.
- We have great love for your society and each of you individually.
- See yourself smiling everyday in the mirror of physical reality.
- A world that still believes it's the only human life-form in existence.

About the Authors

Chapter 1

Arvantis Discovers Life on Earth

"We walk, we breathe, we sleep, we dream, and we eat together. We value life and one another and we nurture one another in all ways that we can at all times. We are always growing, sharing, educating, understanding, communicating, lovingly, and enrichingly. Those then are perhaps the most valuable things in our culture. The greatest value to us!"

- Arvantis

December 22nd, 2009

{*…This chapter begins with Group of Friends being channeled by Shaun…*}

Group of Friends: Very well then, here we are! As we like to say in your frame of reference, on a warm, blustery, windy, December 22nd day in your year as you count calendar years, 2009. We will facilitate this conversation between you and that which you understand as a feline lifetime of your soul aspect, of that energy which you will most be connected with in your current physical incarnation.

Jefferson: Nice.

Group of Friends: How now would you like to begin this afternoon of our interaction together?

Jefferson: How is this communication with my feline future-self going to happen? Am I going to talk to him directly? Is he there with you?

{ *...Jefferson's feline future-self steps into the channeling frequency with the assistance of Group of Friends and he answers Jefferson's questions in the following way...* }

Future-Self: Yes, and I am he!

Jefferson: Oh, great! I thought I was talking to Ishuwa. So...can you tell me...I want to know...do you live in a physical world like we do?

Future-Self: I do, yes!

Jefferson: My first question is how tall are you?

Future-Self: Approximately six-and-a-half feet of your Earth's measurements.

Jefferson: Six what?

Future-Self: Six-and-a-half feet.

Jefferson: Oh, so you are tall!

Future-Self: You take one of your feet and you add it six times and you cut a seventh one in half! I am six and a half feet!

Jefferson: Okay.

Future-Self: Yes!

Jefferson: And are you a boy or a girl?

Future-Self: I am of a male orientation.

Jefferson: Okay, and what's your coloration?

Future-Self: A little bit of a light blue coloration, primarily.

Jefferson: Do you have big eyes?

Future-Self: I do!

Jefferson: Are they cat eyes?

Future-Self: No.

Jefferson: They are human eyes?

Future-Self: A little bit of a mixture of how you would see cat eyes and human eyes. A little bit of a mixing. Kind of a half-and-half.

Jefferson: Nice.

Future-Self: But our pupils tend to be oriented more in the way that you are familiar with in the humans on your world.

Jefferson: Are your ears more like a cat or more like a human?

Future-Self: They're more like a human.

Jefferson: Oh.

Future-Self: Over to the side of the skull…not on top of the head.

Jefferson: Does it remind…it's a bit different, right?

Future-Self: In what sense are you asking "different?"

Jefferson: Are there some feline aspects to it?

Future-Self: A little bit, sure. A little bit of a point, more so than generally found on your world.

Jefferson: Hmm.

Future-Self: But it isn't all furry. It doesn't have quite the same amount of open to the exterior world in terms of a cat's ears being very open.

Jefferson: Oh, I see. And do you have a nose or a muzzle?

Future-Self: More like a nose.

Jefferson: And you have teeth?

Future-Self: Yes.

Jefferson: Well, then you are a human!

Future-Self: But they aren't sharp and pointy like a cat on your world.

Jefferson: Okay, well that's interesting! And what's the color of your eyes?

Future-Self: A little bit of a green coloration and a little bit of yellow as well.

Jefferson: Okay.

Future-Self: A very iridescent green, very much like you would find in a forest in the Amazon region. A very brilliant green!

Jefferson: That's nice. Now, we are both the same soul, right?

Future-Self: From one perspective you could say that.

Jefferson: Are you in what I would consider my future?

Future-Self: Yes.

Jefferson: How far in the future?

Future-Self: About 357 years.

Jefferson: Wow. Okay, so are you my future self?

Future-Self: One!

Jefferson: All right. What's the name of your solar system or galaxy?

Future-Self: OrOctal.

Jefferson: How do you spell that?

Future-Self: O, r, O, c, t, a, l.

Jefferson: Okay, and what's the name of your planet?

Future-Self: At this time we will refer to it as Revision number 5!

Jefferson: Okay. And what does that mean?

Future-Self: That is the name that we will refer to it by at this time for your ability to talk about it with us, to have some label to identify it by.

Jefferson: I see.

Future-Self: There is another term, another label we also refer to it by that is closer to our native label and in time we will share that with you.

Jefferson: Great.

Future-Self: But if you want to talk about our planet for now, so we know what you are referring to, you can call it Revision 5 or Revision #5, either way!

Jefferson: Revision 5.

Future-Self: Yes! That is a world of ours in our solar system, OrOctal.

Jefferson: Octo...?

Future-Self: OrOctal.

Jefferson: And what is the name of your civilization?

Future-Self: We are the Arkoreuns, and again, our solar system is OrOctal, the planet is Revision 5.

Jefferson: Okay, Arkoreuns! Do you look like me?

Future-Self: I do not!

Jefferson: Do you have hair?

Future-Self: Yes.

Jefferson: How so?

Future-Self: From the scalp, the hair follicles are thick, but we don't have a lot of hair growing out of the scalp, only a sparse amount. What we do have is thick. It is a dark brown that almost appears black.

Jefferson: Is it long?

Future-Self: Along the back, for some, yes!

Jefferson: And for you?

Future-Self: For me, no.

Jefferson: How long is your hair?

Future-Self: Just past the neckline.

Jefferson: Well, that's long.

Future-Self: If you say so.

Jefferson: Okay. How do you comb it? Do you comb it?

Future-Self: It takes care of itself very well, thank you!

Jefferson: Where are you physically located right now?

Future-Self: I am in a region of my OrOctal solar system, and I am on my planet Revision 5.

Jefferson: Okay. What is your society's relationship with ours?

Future-Self: We have found your world to be most interesting. There are a number of you that are connected with us genetically. We enjoy sharing this home coming experience with you in whatever way we find we can.

Jefferson: By your description, you really look like humans.

Future-Self: Very much so from our perspective because we are familiar with many varieties of shapes, and colors, and sizes of humans. But in your world, your people would not see us as a human. We would appear quite different. We would feel quite different to you. Your mind would function quite differently in our presence because you haven't had much interaction with extraterrestrial humans.

Jefferson: Hmm.

Future-Self: You have only seen a very small portion of the number, and styles, and varieties of humans that exist.

Jefferson: How many planets are there in your solar system?

Future-Self: We have approximately fourteen.

Jefferson: Oh, fourteen, I thought so. And how many Suns?

Future-Self: One Sun.

Jefferson: And do you have what we have…something like a moon?

Future-Self: We have seven on Revision 5.

Jefferson: Wow.

Future-Self: They aren't quite like the one you have on your world. There are three of them that rotate around a fourth one. They are almost like a small solar system unto theirself. The other three are following one another very closely, sometimes quite invisible to us from our planet's surface. Sometimes we can see them as separate, distinct moons. They aren't as large as the one on your world. They don't have as much of an impact on gravitation as the one on your world does.

Jefferson: What are they for?

Future-Self: They are to experience life in the ways they choose with us, for they are living beings as well. They are of a different form, and shape, and consciousness, yes, but they don't necessarily need to be there for any reason to sustain our existence. Simply that we have all chosen to coexist in that way, in that form, to have moons of seven around our planet. They chose our planet to orbit around for their own reasons.

Jefferson: Okay, what about the Sun?

Future-Self: We have that yes. It isn't quite as large as yours. It is much younger. It is able to emanate more heat, in a sense, more light, in a sense, more energy, in a sense, and it serves us beautifully.

Jefferson: And does your planet, Revision 5, does it rotate around the Sun?

Future-Self: Yes.

Jefferson: What does your planet look like?

Future-Self: It is a very green planet. A little bit of rivers here and there. Not as much ocean as you have on Earth. We have a similar atmosphere. Not quite as expansive as the one on your Earth. We are able to enter the region you would call space much sooner, for our atmosphere doesn't rise as high as the one on your world does from the planet's surface. The oxygen is a little bit different, and it is certainly what we would consider to be more toxin-free, more sustaining. It isn't quite as dense as what it once was on Earth, but due to its purity, in that sense, it is able to sustain us very well.

Jefferson: And...do you guys wear clothes?

Future-Self: We do have a variety of fashions, in that sense, yes.

Jefferson: Do you live in the forest?

Future-Self: There are some who do.

Jefferson: How about yourself?

Future-Self: I have a residence in what you would call a forest. Similar to what you would know as the Amazonas on your world. It doesn't have quite as many of the creatures that you have, the living organisms in your Amazonas region. It is, in a sense, more friendly to our co-existence with it. We are able to be there and not have to be concerned about any unusual animals or insects that might inflict some unusual energies upon us or want to feed upon us. That does not occur.

Jefferson: And at night, are there flowers that glow?

Future-Self: Glowing flowers?

Jefferson: Yeah.

Future-Self: There is a region in what you would consider the North portion of the planet that does have a variety of flowers. Some are very similar to those on your world. There are others quite different as far as those that seem to glow. We have a few that appear to glow even in full mid-day sunshine and then at night they seem to disappear. But at night we generally don't have what you would call glowing flowers.

We do have some flowers that at night can attract a particular pigment, a particular form of life that is quite colorful and can give off the effect of a glowing flower, but it isn't the flower itself that contains the glowing quality. It is that pigment, the living organism that resides on the flower's surface that is of the glowing energy and light source.

Jefferson: And how well do you see at night?

Future-Self: Very well! I have ability with my vision that functions very well at night.

Jefferson: Oh, that is true, you are feline.

Future-Self: What we see in the night is quite different than what we are able to visualize in the daylight. Generally, as the Sun is setting, there is an internal mechanism that will have our vision adjust to a bit more in depth ability to take in the surrounding environment in a way that allows us to see things at night more clearly than perhaps humans on your world are able to visualize. Based on our observation, most in your world seem to be unable to see as much at night, unless there is some artificial light present to light their way, so to speak.

Jefferson: Hmm.

Future-Self: We have grown up on this world with this mechanism in our genetic structure, so it is very natural for us to be able to see things at night even when the moons are not above in the sky.

Jefferson: Wow. That's very interesting!

Future-Self: We find it to be so too!

Jefferson: Is your bone structure stronger than ours?

Future-Self: Well, it is a different structure. The skeletal structure is similar to yours, but the material, the composite components are of a different nature. A little bit different patterning in the way in which they form and this provides them with what you would consider a stronger impact resistance. You could say stronger, but it is a different material that is serving a similar function.

Jefferson: And what do you eat?

Future-Self: We have a variety of foods. Some we grow, as you do on your world with agriculture. Others we find abundantly within nature, and there are things that you would probably classify as fruits and vegetables. There are forms of food that are like a seed that we enjoy immensely as well.

Jefferson: Hmm.

Future-Self: We don't consume other life forms on our planet that you on your world would consider poultry and beef. At times will have some forms of food available to us in the rivers that would be a little bit like a fish, but it has more of a component in which it grows in the river. So it develops from the soil beneath the water's surface, more like a fruit or vegetable does, but it is more similar in flavoring as you would find fish in your world to be.

Jefferson: And...can you swim?

Future-Self: I have that ability, yes.

Jefferson: And...are you guys able to teleport?

Future-Self: We have the ability to move about from our planet's surface to other locations off planet or to other locations on planet. This ability is like a teleportation system.

Jefferson: Oh! It's a teleportation system like an elevator from one place to another. It's not like you can do that alone with your body only?

Future-Self: We do have ability to move about without the technical construct that you would think of being like an elevator.

Jefferson: So you disappear from one place and appear in another?

Future-Self: That is a component usually we use only for inter-planetary travel.

Jefferson: Ahhhh. Why?

Future-Self: Because it takes a lot longer to travel distances if we use a mechanical mode that you might think of being like a flying saucer.

Jefferson: Oh.

Future-Self: We have crafts that are shaped like what you typically consider to be a flying saucer, but our crafts are more like a conscious light-ship, and we are able then with that conscious craft to move about very quickly. Sometimes we use that form of travel on the surface of our planet, but usually we have other modes of transportation for our surface travels, for travel upon our planet.

Jefferson: So for you, if you want to go from one place to another, say one city to another, would you...you don't teleport?

Future-Self: No, generally we don't, but we do have that ability. We do have some of that infrastructure, generally reserved for people who are visiting us, but at times we will use it ourself. People from other planets who travel differently, we will at times then use it for them and with them.

Jefferson: Oh, I see. So what you are saying is that sometimes you are going to use the technology that you have on your planet to go from one place to another because of the visitors, but you yourself for example, if you want to go to another city on your planet, you can't teleport your body there?

Future-Self: Generally, we don't teleport our body. We enjoy traveling on foot, and we find that to be a more enjoyable mode of transportation. Our world isn't as large as yours so we don't have as much surface to cover.

Jefferson: Oh!

Future-Self: We don't generally want to get somewhere really fast. We are able to communicate with those in other regions of the planet through a form of telepathy and then we are able to see what they are seeing, in a sense, through our mind's eye. You might understand that idea.

Jefferson: Hmm.

Future-Self: That enables us, in a sense, to join in with them in another location on the planet's surface without actually physically going there, but we can get into a teleportation device if we feel it's absolutely necessary. It does occur at times, even if we don't have guests from another world visiting with us.

Jefferson: Okay.

Future-Self: Generally we travel with our feet. We are quite capable of moving fast over long distances for an extended period of time, and we enjoy such journeys, such form of traveling.

Jefferson: And...do you have a house in a tree?

Future-Self: I do not. Some do. I reside on the surface in what you would consider a home structure. It's generally formed out of some of the plants that grow quite abundantly on our world. We shape and fashion an abode or house structure out of this form of organic plant matter.

Jefferson: Is it anything like houses we have?

Future-Self: It serves a similar purpose. We reside in it. However, we don't have a lot of wires, and switches, and individual wall separations, and bathroom facilities, and sinks, and showers, and garbage disposals, and things of that sort built inside. It's more of a large room, more of what you would find in a Native American teepee, in that sense, a large open space.

Jefferson: And do you come back home everyday? Do you sleep at home every night?

Future-Self: Frequently, but at times I am not on planet. If I am on planet, then usually I will.

Jefferson: Are you the only son?

Future-Self: I have four that are of my family, from my parents. That makes me the fifth!

Jefferson: Are they all males or females?

Future-Self: There are three female and two male.

Jefferson: Are you the youngest or the oldest?

Future-Self: I am of the oldest of the male and the youngest after the other three female.

Jefferson: So you are the child number 2?

Future-Self: There are three sisters older than I, and I am older than my brother.

Jefferson: Good…brother…sure…that's exciting! Now, can you tell us about a type of transportation that you have? You have spoken about the spacecrafts, but what else? Do you have buses?

Future-Self: No.

Jefferson: Do you have pets?

Future-Self: No.

Jefferson: You don't have pets?

Future-Self: You sound surprised!

Jefferson: Well, they are fun.

Future-Self: Very well, perhaps you can bring us one.

Jefferson: Yeah! Well, I'm not sure about that. Can I survive on the surface of your planet?

Future-Self: There would be an enormous amount of adjustment necessary for that to be something you could do. It would take several months of adjustment given where you are presently at your physical frequency.

Jefferson: Hmm.

Future-Self: But after the adjustment, which we would be able to oversee, then you would be able to. There is another way in which we would have, in a sense, an energetic field around you. It would allow you to be present on the planet without the transition, the becoming more climatized to the surface, but we wouldn't be able to remove the field until you had climatized. Once you climatized, you would be able to move about similar to how we do. And you could do so without any real dire affects on your being.

Jefferson: And if I had that shield around my body, I wouldn't be able to hug you guys would I?

Future-Self: Thank you for thinking of hugging us.

Jefferson: Well, is that possible?

Future-Self: We would be able to do that energetically in a way that you would find most enjoyable as a hug in which you find joy in that action in your world.

Jefferson: Talking about joy, how do you grow up?

Future-Self: Very slowly and enjoyably.

Jefferson: Okay. Can you tell me any details about your childhood?

Future-Self: I became conscious of my surroundings at approximately one-and-a-half months after my birthing.

Jefferson: Okay.

Future-Self: My birthing wasn't that different from how you are born in your world. I was able to begin moving about after approximately three to four months. I speak of myself, but in general for those of my world, it is at three to four months that we begin having the ability to move about, to stand, to walk, to be able to be self-sufficient in terms of mobility—

Jefferson: Hmm.

Future-Self: —three to four months. From there, back to my own personal experience, I had what you would think of as three sisters and we would then go about the idea of what you would consider play in what you would consider a neighborhood where there were others who were nearby. Not as close as you generally find in cities on your world. We don't have that type of neighborhood on our world, no close, densely populated cities. We tend to have our homes more spaced apart.

Jefferson: Okay.

Future-Self: We would find, amongst our own family, opportunities as a child growing up to go out in the neighborhood and to, what you would think of as play, which we were very excited by, enjoyed doing when growing up at that early age.

There were frequent meetings with our parents and with the parents of others who set up community gatherings. Frequently we still get together as a community so that there is a oneness of mind and feeling, a cohesive consciousness on our world that allows us to communicate harmoniously, upliftingly in all that we do together. And when we are on our own and venturing about, journeying and exploring on our own or in smaller groups, whatever size, we have some individual meetings. Not as a large community but in smaller groups we would have. I would have.

I would join in particular groups that I felt would have topics, teachings, sharings that I would be most interested in so I could learn things that were attracted to me and I was attracted to. It was as though I chose my school curriculum in that way. I wasn't told that I had to go to this class or that class and study this or that. If I wasn't interested in something, I wouldn't attend those groups or those meetings while I was growing up. This affords us the opportunity to be learning and growing while developing and nurturing a cohesive bonding with our community as a whole. We learn in an individual way and bond with the whole. I learned that which I enjoyed, what was attractive to me along the way. That is some of what I remain aware of from what you would have called growing up.

Jefferson: Okay! What have you chosen to study in this lifetime?

Future-Self: I work with what you would call a form of life sciences. I interact with organic life forms and study the physiologies of life forms such as plants and humans. I study components of the biology and the understandings that exist within the biologies. I study the different systems that afford any life form its bodily being. For instance, if you were referring to a human being on Earth, I would study aspects of their biology, their cardiovascular system, their neurological system, study along those lines.

Jefferson: Hmm.

Future-Self: Not as a medical doctor that you have on your world. I would be learning and studying the life on more of an energetic component or level. Understanding how the different systems in the body function and relate to one another, communicate with one another from a more organic place.

Jefferson: That is something I like to do! What a coincidence! How long can you live in your body?

Future-Self: About 200 years, there can be variations.

Jefferson: And how old are you?

Future-Self: I am about seventy-three.

Jefferson: Seventy-three.

Future-Self: On my world, approximately seventy-three.

Jefferson: And would you be able to make the translation of numbers to my world?

Future-Self: That would be approximately one-third.

Jefferson: Oh, somewhere in the twenties, about twenty-five or so. And...do you remember any game that you played that was fun?

Future-Self: Oh, they are all fun!

Jefferson: They are all fun.

Future-Self: I don't recall any that I didn't have fun doing.

Jefferson: No?

Future-Self: I do remember some that began to be of less interest to me and I would then remove myself from that game.

Jefferson: What game have you played that you think I would find fun?

Future-Self: That you would find fun?

Jefferson: Yes!

Future-Self: Well, that would be for you to decide.

Jefferson: Okay. Have you…do you play any sports?

Future-Self: I do not. We do not have sports as you have on your world.

Jefferson: Do you have an equivalent?

Future-Self: We do not.

Jefferson: Well, okay. Do you have arts?

Future-Self: We do have forms of artistic expression. Some…not painting or sculpture. We generally have a form of group song and individual song. Generally without words. It is generally more like a chanting but with far less the repetition that you can find often in your world's chants. For us it tends to be quite spontaneous.

Jefferson: How do you communicate with each other?

Future-Self: We have the ability to talk vocally and telepathically. We do both. Our language, of course, is different than what we are speaking with you now.

Jefferson: What's the name of your language?

Future-Self: You can refer to it as an Arkoreun language.

Jefferson: Okay. Do you grow more than six-and-a-half feet in height?

Future-Self: I will probably grow in the range of seven to seven-and-a-half feet within the next five years.

Jefferson: And are you aware of the transition that is happening on Earth as far as consciousness goes?

Future-Self: I am! We are!

Jefferson: And, when was the...when was the first time that you heard of me?

Future-Self: I was very young. Approximately five. I was viewing some records of Earth in our archive.

Jefferson: Hmm.

Future-Self: I found myself viewing some records of what you would refer to as you in your current incarnation. I didn't know the records were of you and viewing them seemed very strange to me for some reason. So then I asked about it with those who are understanding of such experiences and they then were able to guide me in a way that I was able to discover for myself who you were. I realized why I was feeling what I did when I was observing these visual archives. That then at five was how I came to be aware of who you are. But you were at a different age in the archive I viewed than what you are now.

Jefferson: What age was I in the archive?

Future-Self: You were in your seventh birthday.

Jefferson: Okay, can you tell me more about that day? What did you feel when you saw me? What exactly happened?

Future-Self: Initially, I was guided from within to view a particular era of your Earth, a particular region of your world, and just...you could say I coincidentally came upon a "channel," a visual of that which I later learned it was you but upon initial viewing I was feeling rather disoriented which was something unfamiliar to me. So I stepped aside from the viewing to consult with those educators who were present to guide me to understand why I was feeling disoriented. Was I…was there something wrong with the visual in the archive that was causing my disorientation I asked?

Jefferson: And?

Future-Self: They assured me that was not what was taking place. There was nothing wrong with the visual archive, rather I was going through a connection, a remembrance of some sort that was important for me to understand, to realize. They then gave me some exercises to do that allowed me to, in a sense, remember who you were. It was more that I just connected to a "knowing" of who you were. That then afforded me the opportunity to begin a gradual process of communicating to you at various times that seemed most conducive for building a relationship at this timing and in this fashion, in this format that we and I are communicating with you in now.

Jefferson: What…when you went to talk to them, what did they tell you about me?

Future-Self: I was the one who came to know who you were. They merely observed my process of coming into that realizational process. They guided me through how to understand, how to remember who you were. To know who you were.

Jefferson: And what exercise did they give you?

Future-Self: They asked me to imagine that I was that person and to then imagine that I was seeing the surroundings that person in the visual archives was seeing and to place my resonance of being in that person's body, so to speak, to do so imaginarily. That was the main technique. There were some other subtle techniques, what you might think of as meditative techniques to calm the body, to calm the breathing, to calm the pulsing of the heart, to calm the surrounding environment that I am in —

Jefferson: Hmm.

Future-Self: —so that it would be easier for me to place myself imaginarily into a resonance with the person that I was visually viewing in the archive. In that way, over a period of time, I began tuning into the consciousness of that person, of that you, and because you then had grown some and had come to know more about who you were and where you were, I began experiencing that understanding as well, as if the knowingness you had was also the knowingness that I had. I retained that and then came back into a full awareness of myself in the room where I was viewing the visual archive.

Jefferson: Okay.

Future-Self: Eventually I was able to observe you. Knowing that I was you in that time frame, I was able to move forward from there to learn more about what that meant, why I came into that contact in that way. Those who were present in my world, like educators or teachers, were then able to guide me further in how to progress, how to move forward in the connection with you!

Jefferson: And when you realized why you had come across that archive, what was the reason?

Future-Self: It is quite multi-layered, but the primary thing is to help you be in a position to facilitate your own growth and those of others in the ways that you would find enjoyable to do so. To share information that can be a vital link for others to realize more of who they are, in that sense. To, if you will metaphorically, step out of the "jungle of insects and animals" that prey upon the deeper understandings of who you all really are, in a sense, so people can become more aware and self empowered as the creators of the reality they experience. Do you follow that idea?

Jefferson: I do! And it is fascinating! You said that you started communicating with me. When was the first communication that we had?

Future-Self: You were approximately seven. That experience of mine that I just described was a form of communication to you too. You had some unusual experiences in that time as well. As I began to understand what was occurring, as I began to feel like I was in resonance with your being, seeing your surroundings, understanding then in that way who you were by simply experiencing with you as you were experiencing that moment in your life, I began — because I grew into the awareness of what was occurring with me — I began letting you know what was occurring.

Jefferson: Oh.

Future-Self: Letting you know that I was there and who I was. To the best of my ability, I explained to you who I was and that I would be in contact with you again at some point when you would be more in a position and of interest to know more about me.

Jefferson: And when was our second communication?

Future-Self: You had a dream some days later in which you were wanting to know what had happened in that first moment that I was resonating synchronistically with you and ultimately communicated with you that first time. That is, you were in your dream state exploring the unusual experiences you had had a few days before when I had first been present there with you.

Jefferson: I missed some of what you just said. Can you repeat?

Future-Self: You, in a dream state a few days later, began exploring and wanting to know what had happened and why you had had the first unusual experiences —

Jefferson: Okay.

Future-Self: —and in that dream exploration I was able to contact you for the second time. I let you know basically the same thing that I told you the first time. That I was there visiting you and that I would meet up with you again sometime in your future if you so felt inclined or attracted to doing so—

Jefferson: Okay.

Future-Self: —that it would be something you could do! That was the basic idea, the basic information given to you in that dream. That was the second meeting we had, from my perception, that I am presently aware of.

Jefferson: So do you think that because we are the same soul, would it be possible to have a transfer of consciousness in which you would be able to experience life through my physical body and I would experience life through your physical body?

Future-Self: This can occur!

Jefferson: Hmm. Has it occurred before?

Future-Self: In your dream states, yes!

Jefferson: Oh, okay. So what you mean is, in my dream state I have visited you in your world.

Future-Self: Yes!

Jefferson: And why don't I remember?

Future-Self: You will in appropriate timing.

Jefferson: Okay. I want to ask if you know about the transition in the consciousness level of humanity that is going on now because we are definitely growing—

Future-Self: One moment…

Jefferson: Yes.

Future-Self: There are things you do remember, you just don't understand that they come from having visited me in my world.

Jefferson: Such as what?

Future-Self: You have things that come to mind that you aren't aware of how to place them. You don't have a context, a frame of reference that allows you to identify those experiences, those moments as being connected to when you were visiting me on my world.

Jefferson: Wow! So from your perspective, when I visit you in my dream state, once I get there, do I look physical?

Future-Self: Yes!

Jefferson: And what does my physical body look like?

Future-Self: That which you are presently in your physical.

Jefferson: The same physical body size and the same proportions, everything?

Future-Self: Yes.

Jefferson: And when was my last visit?

Future-Self: That would be approximately three-and-a-half years ago.

And what did we do?

Future-Self: We went out to one of the local community rivers and explored in a gathering amongst others who were like yourself, visiting from their world. It was like a group event of beings from several planets that were beginning to become more comfortable with understanding and accepting that there are extraterrestrials in the Universe. It is a form of climatizing yourself to that reality by being with others from other worlds in this group gathering and seeing other life forms in this group setting. That would have been about three-and-a-half years ago as you count time.

Jefferson: And...did I give you a hug?

Future-Self: In a matter of speaking, yes!

Jefferson: So then...you basically know what I look like exactly because I have visited you.

Future-Self: You know exactly what I look like too. You just have yet to remember.

Jefferson: Okay. And...I was referring earlier to the level of consciousness on Earth, as we are growing and emerging into a way of seeing the world as a greater community of intelligence, is it possible that I will be able to physically visit you?

Future-Self: This may occur, yes! More likely we will physically visit you first though.

Jefferson: Is your race the second race that will be in contact with us after the Yahyel?

Future-Self: We don't have a line up, in that sense, a number. That will be decided as the initial contacts occur. It is possible we could be, but it isn't something that is, in that sense, written in stone.

Jefferson: Okay! If you were to read the energy where I stand right now, in how many years do you think it could potentially happen that I will meet you physically?

Future-Self: It could be about twenty to thirty-five.

Jefferson: That's it?

Future-Self: That's not long at all, is it.

No, I mean...when I have the vision of that waiting for me...I mean, it's worthy of waiting for.

Future-Self: I agree.

Jefferson: But...okay. What mechanisms can I use to go and visit someone like you, my future self for example? What can a human use to visit their future self more in the dreamtime?

Future-Self: Well, simply having the desire to do so. Before you go to sleep, you can voice that desire. You can write about it. You can think about it. You can have ceremony about it. Create your own ceremony in your house, or outdoors in the woods, or in a park, or at the beach, or at the lake, or at a river. Expressing your intention to create a stronger connection in dream states and in the physical as well. The more you put out that intention, the more it will facilitate ability for you to remember as you awaken each day the dreams and connections that you have with us.

Jefferson: Wow! Now, I would like to ask you, what is your name?

Future-Self: Arvantis.

Jefferson: Wow! You have to spell it for me.

Future-Self: A, r, v, a, n, t, i, s, would be a good written form.

Jefferson: A, r, v, a, n, t, i, s?

Future-Self: Yes.

Jefferson: And how do people on your world pronounce your name?

Future-Self: Arvantis. {...*from this point forward in the book, "Arvantis" will be used instead of "Future-Self" to indicate when Jefferson's feline future-self is talking...*}

Jefferson: And do you guys have a parent's name after your first name? I don't think you have that.

Arvantis: I am not named after my father or mother or their father or their mother. There is no one in my family that has this type of name. Generally that is so for all others on my world.

Jefferson: And what does your name mean?

Arvantis: It is simply a name that I find most attractive. It relates to the rivers flowing through a wooded region of the world where I live that I find most at home for me to be in and so it's something in that place of enjoyment that I was in that the name came to me. And so you could say it doesn't really translate into any particular meaning, only that for me it means the idea of being in that space, in that place with the rivers soothingly flowing through the wooded area that I find most at home when I am in that space.

Jefferson: So in your society a person gives him or herself their own name?

Arvantis: In my case yes, but not all the time. Not in every instance. It is up to the child to decide if the parents or someone else in the family will provide the name. Sometimes it can be someone outside of the family, but the child will know and choose who it will be. Often it will be the child themself that will make the decision but not always.

Jefferson: And until you decide your name, how do they refer to you?

Arvantis: They simply know who we are, for we communicate telepathically. We all have our unique conscious connection, vibrational signature, resonance of embodiment, and we are able to communicate simply to get each other's attention, simply with that knowingness, beingness. We don't really use names in that way that you do in your world.

Jefferson: Okay! And do you grow older?

Arvantis: Yes.

Jefferson: Physically?

Arvantis: Yes.

Jefferson: Do you enjoy that?

Arvantis: It is a part of the experience I enjoy.

Jefferson: Are there physical changes as you grow older?

Arvantis: We have that yes. We don't generally have the physical lessening of strength as you may find in your world. No illness or handicap as a result of an illness that could in your world's experience remove the body's ability to optimally function.

Jefferson: Hmm.

Arvantis: We might, as we get older, slow down a little bit in our pace, but this would be more from a state of that person's mind rather than the physical body's ability. We can move quite actively at our last day, even if you were to live to be 200 years old. We generally just don't move about as quickly at that age through our own choice to move more slowly.

Jefferson: Oh, I see.

Arvantis: You will not find us in wheelchairs or with walkers. Not even on our 200th birthday.

Jefferson: And you are bipedal, of course, you are just like a human right? You stand like a human!

Arvantis: Yes, very similar physiologically.

Jefferson: How many fingers do you have?

Arvantis: Same number as on your world.

Jefferson: Oh my! And for the feet as well?

Arvantis: Yes, same number of toes. Some of us only have four toes including the big toe. Some have five.

Jefferson: And on the hand as well, you have five fingers?

Arvantis: Yes, a thumb and four fingers.

Jefferson: I see!

Arvantis: It could be referred to as five fingers.

Jefferson: Yeah. Okay. Well, it's been lovely this first interaction with you in this manner.

Arvantis: Most lovely with you in this manner as well. Certainly a joy to have this first engaging conversation with you in this way to guide us together in this relationship in a more conscious way for both of us. Certainly for you too, given that most contact you have had with me up to this point has been through others or through your dream state. So it's a great celebration to have the doors of communication opening with you in this way, for you are an aspect of me and I of you. It is a wondrous celebration! A festive moment! I assure you those in our world who are present in this opening with you, and expansion of our awareness of one another, and ability to communicate with one another, we are going to be celebrating for a few days to come.

Jefferson: And I will celebrate in my heart too! This is so fascinating, and the story that your shared earlier about that archive that you came across…that was outstanding!

Arvantis: We have an audience member that is asking a question.

Jefferson: Okay. Who is it?

Hi Jefferson, hi Arvantis, this is Sheridan. I am here in the room with the channel, Shaun. I have one question and that is, in your culture what do your people value the most? What are your values?

Arvantis: We value our life and that of All That Is. For all life is us. We value then those who are present in our experience, our journey, and our life each moment. We value then those that are most present in our life at any given moment, those who are physically present and energetically present. We have a deep appreciation with one another, for one another. That then is perhaps our primary value. There are many others but that perhaps would be one of the most predominant ones that we are born with, and grow up with, and are taught. We experience others in our world valuing each other and life itself.

These values serve as a model for the young ones and this is a model that does not ever break. It does not ever get lost. It does not ever lose its brilliance, its luminous quality, nor its importance in our culture. We walk, we breathe, we sleep, we dream, we eat together. We value life and one another and we nurture one another in all ways that we can at all times. We are always growing, sharing, educating, understanding, communicating, lovingly, and enrichingly. Those then are perhaps the most valuable things in our culture. The greatest values to us. Thank you for the question!

Thank you!

Jefferson: Arvantis, can you ask someone now that is around you there if they have any questions for me?

Arvantis: One moment.

{...after a few moments of silence...}

Arvantis: What is your favorite pastime?

Jefferson: I like to study a lot. Some people don't call that a pastime in our world, but I enjoy learning. I like to study and get a hold of new concepts and ideas so...not only that, but the discipline of study helps me free myself from old ideas that don't serve me anymore and this supports my ability to teach other people as well.

Arvantis: Lovely. Could you be more specific for fellow attendees what you mean by a lot, what would a lot be, share one or two ideas of that thing you study a lot?

Jefferson: When I say a lot...I mean when I am not working...I am dedicating myself to learning more and being really focused and...

Arvantis: The question, more specifically is, what topics do you study a lot of, what themes? Do you study about trees or birds a lot, or do you study about planets a lot?

Jefferson: About human consciousness and our connection with All That Is.

Arvantis: Very well!

Jefferson: Metaphysics!

Arvantis: Yes! And what then do you find most fascinating at the current time in your studying of human consciousness? Anything you would like to share with those who are attending with us?

Jefferson: What I find most fascinating in humans is that we are able to forget who we truly are and yet within this forgetful state of being we are able to give a hand of assistance to others in need. Also, we are able to embrace and assist one another in many instances when the "life-grip" is tough and we can laugh even though many things are telling us that there is no reason to laugh. This is what I find most fascinating about the idea of the human at this point.

Arvantis: Thank you for sharing that! Yes! Very well then. We understand you would like to have more of these kinds of conversations for a book you are putting together. If that is so, then we are most delighted to continue on with you in this manner at another time which you would call a future day.

Jefferson: Sure!

Arvantis: Does that fit with you?

Jefferson: Yes!

Arvantis: Very well then! We thank you. Are there any other questions before we depart this moment of your day?

Jefferson: Who asked the question?

Arvantis: That would be one of those in my family. That would be my youngest sister who is older than I.

Jefferson: Oh, how nice! Tell her I thank her very much for being present.

Arvantis: She is most welcoming of your thankfulness, and thank you as well for your interest to move forward in this way!

Jefferson: Lovely! Thank you very much.

Arvantis: You are welcome! Thank you. Until we meet again in this format, much love to you young dear soooooul reflection of myself!

Jefferson: Yes! Much love to you all too!

Chapter 2

Uncovering the Real World of Human ETs

"We have all the strength we need just by following and doing what is of greatest joy for us to do. Our genetic structure always supports this form of existence for us."

- Arvantis

December 23rd, 2009

Arvantis: Very well! A joy to be here with you in this moment! How are you?

Jefferson: Delighted to have the opportunity to speak to you again!

Arvantis: Yes, a delight as well for me and us, to have this interaction with you as well. What is it on your mind today that you would like to share with us in this moment together?

Jefferson: Can you tell us what you have done since we last spoke yesterday?

Arvantis: I am simply relaxing in the sunshine. Taking in a little bit of the day, in that sense. Celebrating with those who are here and simply being together and holding space, as it were, for the communication we have in this process with you. Honoring the opening, celebration of the connection, a reawakening, a reconnecting with you in this fashion. All of this is like a ceremony, just taking in the day, enjoying the sunshine together in honor of this awakening and opening and new adventure together in this format.

Jefferson: How did you come to know that I wanted to communicate with you in these ways?

Arvantis: We listen! We hear you! You have a link, a communication link with us already established. You just haven't been aware of it.

Jefferson: How so?

Arvantis: You speak. You have an idea, and we hear that when it's directed towards us.

Jefferson: Oh, okay! So you were hearing a lot last night?

Arvantis: We hear some. Not all.

Jefferson: Where are you right now?

Arvantis: I am still on the planet Revision 5, our home planet. A wonderful place.

Jefferson: Can you describe your surroundings?

Arvantis: I am outdoors in what is like a meadow that has some short growth of plant matter in a very soft soil. Surrounding that are some very large trees of various heights. Some five feet, ten feet, fifty, seventy five feet.

Jefferson: Wow.

Arvantis: The meadow is about five hundred feet in diameter although it isn't perfectly round. There are some flowers and some of what you would think of as birds. They are a little bit different but you would consider them birds as that you see in your world. The Sun is up. We don't have clouds at this moment. There is a soft hum that comes from some of the planets here that are in an alignment at this timing. They are together in such an alignment that there is a sound. It's a soft humming, and it is pleasant to hear.

Jefferson: Are you sitting right now? Are you climbing a rock, are you upside down, are you resting on the floor, are you swimming, or are you flying?

Arvantis: I am sitting on a soft soil. You might understand it to be ground, earth, or soil.

Jefferson: Who is there today with you?

Arvantis: We have around me approximately seventeen. Some family and some of those who are holding space. There are others who are aware of this who are attending in another format. My immediate family is present and there are some; what you might think of as relatives. There are some who are recording this and some who are, in a sense, guides who are observing, interacting, taking part as well.

Jefferson: That is now my next question. How does this communication take place from your side?

Arvantis: I have established an ability to communicate with you and there are some others here who hold space. Together on a particular frequency, with our intention, we send information to you and are able then to pick up some of your and the channel's frequencies. In this way, we build a network or link that allows for the communications to be sent from us to you and then from you to us.

Jefferson: Can others hear what I say?

Arvantis: Yes.

Jefferson: Hear in their imagination or hear with their ears?

Arvantis: We have a telepathic link up for them. So there is no speaker system they are listening to.

Jefferson: Can you see me there or just hear?

Arvantis: Presently, we don't have a video camera to watch you in that way. We are able to visualize some of your energy fields, but it wouldn't be something you would be visually familiar with.

Jefferson: As you look at my energy field, what do you see?

Arvantis: We see a few frequencies of a gray around the outer portion of your feet and then, interior wise, there are some yellows and some blues, primarily. A little bit of a green around your forehead area and some pink around your left ear. Your fingers have a little bit of a red around the fingertips. There is in the region of your mid body, your back and your chest, a bit of yellowish green. And there is a vibrant white in the center of your chest region that is also over imposing itself to some degree around your entire body. It is a lighter white emanating from your central chest region. That would be a summary of what we see in that way.

Jefferson: Lovely. So those who are recording this, how are they doing that?

Arvantis: They have some technology that is similar to yours, in that sense of recording, similar to yours.

Jefferson: But we cannot record telepathy.

Arvantis: It isn't necessary to record that. On that level, we are not recording.

Jefferson: Oh, so are you just recording the sound that you make with your voice?

Arvantis: Yes and that which you respond as well, the audio primarily. It is simply something we can playback for others to listen to. The audio recording mechanism picks up some forms of energy that your systems of sound recording there don't pick up yet, but in time they will develop that ability to include some of the energies that our technology does record.

Jefferson: Let's talk about the visual archive that you have of me in your world. How was it recorded?

Arvantis: That was with what you would refer to as orbs in your present world, if you were to see them. They are of a video camera type technology and allow us to take in visual images and record them. They are like a video camera on your world. They come forth into your plane, into your frequency and dimension, appearing often as an orb of light.

Jefferson: Ohhhh, they are those orbs that we see on pictures?

Arvantis: Some, not all are that.

Jefferson: How did you send that orb here?

Arvantis: We do that with our focus of intention for the orb. The camera has some conscious intelligence to it, and it is able to be guided by our intention. We map the location and frequency of where we would like it to go and then, in a sense, it listens, understands, and then goes to that place. And in that space it records visually.

Jefferson: Wow! And then it comes back home.

Arvantis: Yes. In a matter of speaking.

Jefferson: So it's basically a sort of manifestation rather than a traveling?

Arvantis: Yes. It's not like it goes on a long journey like a rocket ship or anything of that sort. We have it, in a sense, move like our spacecraft from one frequency of dimension to another frequency of dimension. From here to there, from this frequency of dimension to the frequency of dimension there. So it doesn't have to travel great distances as you think of traveling distances.

Jefferson: Do you have a television system that allows you to watch what is happening on other planets?

Arvantis: We do, similar to what you have, not completely the same but similar.

Jefferson: Do you have any channel for Earth?

Arvantis: Not a dedicated channel that's on twenty-four seven, so to speak. But there is the ability to connect and link up if there is a need or an educational purpose to it, or to develop a relationship, or to gain an understanding that will further our world's collective growth and upliftment.

Jefferson: So you do have something that would appear like a TV?

Arvantis: Yes. Somewhat like your televisions today.

Jefferson: But if you don't have all those cables in your houses, how do you turn it on?

Arvantis: It would be a little bit more like a wireless technology.

Jefferson: I guess, right!? And, do you have what we would call the written press? Like, magazines, newspapers, books etc.?

Arvantis: We have archives that would be similar, although we don't publish, distribute, and circulate such items as you do in your world.

Jefferson: Have you read anything such as a book?

Arvantis: I have read something that would be like a book in the archive that we have. The language is different. The text is different than what you have.

Jefferson: Hmm.

Arvantis: Different language.

Jefferson: Yeah, because you speak Arkoreun.

Arvantis: Yes.

Jefferson: Sure. Have you written any books?

Arvantis: No, I have not. I have made some contributions to the archive.

Jefferson: I see. Now, is your civilization part of the Association of Worlds?

Arvantis: We do have a connection, yes.

Jefferson: Hmm…How so?

Arvantis: We are one of the multitude that are presently considered members, members through choice. Members having chosen to collaborate and to correspond in this collective association.

Jefferson: And do you know Ishuwa?

Arvantis: I am familiar, yes, with Ishuwa and the Yahyel.

Jefferson: Have they visited your planet?

Arvantis: Yes, this is something that does occur frequently.

Jefferson: So you have met Ishuwa physically?

Arvantis: Yes.

Jefferson: What do they go to your planet for?

Arvantis: For enjoyment! It's something they feel most attracted to doing for their own joyful reasons and in thus doing so we generally will recognize it is a joy for us to have them present, just as when we go there to visit with them.

Jefferson: Oh, you go to their planet?

Arvantis: We have, yes, on occasion.

Jefferson: When was the last time you have been to his planet?

Arvantis: Approximately one-and-a-half weeks of your time.

Jefferson: Isn't he in another timeframe?

Arvantis: Yes. So it would be a different time frame for him, a different time frame for us.

Jefferson: Okay, I guess that doesn't matter then?

Arvantis: Depends on what it is you are focusing on. Whether or not it is important to have that information or not. Whether it will provide you with some more developed understanding of what it is you are experiencing in any given moment.

Jefferson: So the fact that you are in the future gives you a more expanding understanding of what is going on as far as energy?

Arvantis: Relative to your world's present understanding, yes!

Jefferson: And relative to his?

Arvantis: There are some overlaps and there are some differences.

Jefferson: Okay, now let's bring this conversation down to Earth.

Arvantis: Very well.

Jefferson: Has it been of your interest to know how many lifetimes we have had on Earth?

Arvantis: And when you say we, you refer to whom?

The person that you are, me in the future and me here.

Arvantis: How many lifetimes I have had on Earth?

Jefferson: Yeah!

Arvantis: I have had fourteen.

Jefferson: Fourteen?

Arvantis: But they are not all then directly related precisely to the you that you presently are.

Jefferson: But we are the same soul. So one of them is me—

Arvantis: There is a great deal of expansiveness within one soul, such that you can experience a lifetime in a world that I have not and yet we can still be the same soul. And then there are lifetimes you can have where we are both experiencing the same lifetime as well. The soul is such that it does not have to be in the same incarnation everywhere that it exists in the way you perceive the idea of a soul. There are many layers to our soul's existence.

Jefferson: In my understanding, I'm living my present life and at some point in time I will leave this physical body. Then in the future I will incarnate in the Arkoreun race and be you, my future self.

Arvantis: You are now doing that.

Jefferson: Hmm…okay. I would like to explore more of my other lifetime when we communicated and I was Giordano Bruno.

Arvantis: You were then able to talk with me within your own understanding of communicating with your inner mind, your inner dialoguing. It was like a form of channeling internally that you were able to perform in that lifetime. Thus then you didn't have a channel such as the one speaking to you now.

Jefferson: Hmm.

Arvantis: It was as though there was an inner voice within you and I was then being that inner voice having a conversation with you in that way.

Jefferson: And how did it start? Was it during my childhood that we had our first communication in that lifetime?

Arvantis: You had an accident in that lifetime that wasn't really an accident. But it left you in a near death state of mind, state of physiological being that allowed you to let go of many of the "wiring" of belief systems in your mind, crystallized in your brain neurology, such that when you came to, back into your consciousness after the accident, you were then more open to receiving information from me and others. Whoever they may have been. And your wiring belief system was then able to rewire itself with the new connection, the new network, the new channel of communication with me.

Jefferson: How old was I?

Arvantis: You were approximately nineteen.

Jefferson: And you said an accident that wasn't an accident. Can you talk more about that?

Arvantis: Only in the sense that on a deeper level you chose for it, but then that was something you weren't aware of for quite some time in that lifetime. You thought it was an accident for many years. Only in your elder years did you come to the understanding that it was something that you had chosen on a deeper level so that it would allow you to become connected to me and that then it is what occurred. It wasn't really an accident, but initially you perceived it as an accident and those around you did it as well.

Jefferson: And what was it? Did I hit my head or...?

Arvantis: You were accosted by some people who were carrying flames on sticks, torches, and they chased you, and you ran to escape, and you tripped over a ledge and fell down into a gully at night. They couldn't find you nor did they really pursue you for there were others they were then more interested in pursuing that appeared to be more accessible to them, more easy to get a hold of. You had fallen down a slope some fifty meters and they figured you wouldn't be much of life left in you. So they then left you for others. And then some days later those in your community were able to find you, revive you, and gradually bring you back into a nourished and strengthened state of being again.

Jefferson: And when was the first time that I communicated with you?

Arvantis: You had done so at a younger age in that lifetime, well before you were nineteen.

Jefferson: Was it like I did in this lifetime?

Arvantis: Similar, yes. Often in a dream state. But occasionally you would hear words and you would look quickly to the left and the right to see who was there and little hairs on your skin would stand up and you would have a tingling sensation flying about your body. Your heart would pulse quicker, and you would be a bit concerned as to what was happening to you.

Jefferson: Okay, and after the accident that I had in that lifetime when I was nineteen, what was the communication like, what happened?

Arvantis: You began gradually exploring our ability to communicate together without feeling the fear, without looking to the left and the right as you did as a child, without feeling concerned that something was happening to you. You knew that something had happened to you as a result of the fall, and you just took it to heart that you then were somehow different. You chose to go with the flow. You weren't then as frightened of the communication of my voice speaking to you inside your head as you perceived it to be coming from inside your head.

Jefferson: Okay.

Arvantis: In that way we began developing a more natural relationship, communication, conversational ability. Not as frequent as you would with other people in your physical world at that timing. You would set aside time to make the connection much like you do when you make a phone call with someone and you have a conversation with them.

Jefferson: Can I do the same in this lifetime?

Arvantis: You will in time have the ability, but for now there are other things that your mind is working on.

Jefferson: Okay, and what are the main things that we would discuss?

Arvantis: You were interested in how to interact with other people in a way that would give them a greater sense of ease in their life. You wanted to understand how you could have a greater sense of ease in your life. To feel less sense of fear. To help others have a greater sense of joy in their life. To be able to enjoy life more. You were interested in what you could do so you could be in that place of ease. You asked yourself, was it possible to always live in ease? Do people experience such a thing? Was there anyone on Earth who was in a constant state of joy? You had a great deal of curiosity in that idea and then in time you came to recognize it was possible and you began to explore more how you then could have such an experience for yourself with a bit of an overlap of the idea of how you would be able to then help others do the same.

Jefferson: And did I tell you about the difficulties in understanding from the part of the church and people around me?

Arvantis: These were things that were part of the reason you were being chased, if you will, by those with the torches. That had to do with religious indoctrinations, teachings. These were things that you talked about a great deal. It was a very heavy and common topic in the circles that you were interacting with.

Jefferson: Oh, so the torch...I thought they were playing a game. So it wasn't a game? They were unhappy with the things I was saying?

Arvantis: Well, you were part of a community that they were unhappy with so they were trying to frighten you. They were planning and they did capture a few and hold them against their will for a period of a few weeks. A form of torture, but it wasn't very drastic compared with the things that occur in your world today. But the idea was to coerce those people to let go of their ideas and to get back in-line with what most considered to be the appropriate form of thought and living.

Jefferson: And, what else can you tell me about that lifetime as I grew older?

Arvantis: You developed greater understanding of the nature of your existence and how to teach ideas to others. There was some growth in your ability to accept differences about the nature of life, to accept others who had different ideas. There was more understanding by you in the nature and value of allowing for other people to grow in what would be their own appropriate timing. You stopped expecting people to immediately accept the ideas and beliefs about life that you were most attracted to and trying to teach.

You realized others might not accept your ideas and that they might hold on to their ideas for a number of years or even an entire lifetime, thus not accepting anything that you had to offer. You developed a greater sense of tolerance and acceptance for other's ideas no matter how different they were from yours.

It took a while for you to get to the point in that lifetime where you could begin considering accepting what others had to say and acknowledging the value in it. Over time you gained a greater ability to work with that and have more flexibility so that you weren't then preaching to others and telling them that your way was the way it is. You became more open, more flexible in what it was you wanted to share.

Jefferson: And did you influence my writings or way of thinking?

Arvantis: There would be some influence simply from the understandings that we shared in the interacting and communicating together. But it wasn't our purpose, in that sense, then to influence you. That wasn't my purpose.

Jefferson: Sure! And how did you connect with me for the first time? What happened on your side? Could you hear any of the things that I was saying?

Arvantis: After I became aware of your presence through the visualizing I had in the archive when I was approximately five years old, I was then able to tune in to you from time to time, able to hear some things going on with you, not everything, but some of the predominant strongest energies, to get an idea of where you were at and what was taking place, to give me some ideas of what to say and what to share with you.

Jefferson: So in the archive that you saw me in this lifetime when I was seven years old, did you also saw me as Giordano Bruno?

Arvantis: No, there was an adjustment in the idea of linear time. I was not aware of the Giordano Bruno before I connected with you in your present incarnation through the archive viewing.

Jefferson: I see. So...first of all at the age of five you saw me and then you studied a little bit more the idea. You went through the exercises, and when did you get to know about Giordano Bruno?

Arvantis: That would have been for me, really, another lifetime.

Jefferson: Oh, a past life of yours!

Arvantis: Yes.

Jefferson: And you were on the same planet?

Arvantis: Yes.

Jefferson: And do you remember your name?

Arvantis: I do.

Jefferson: Can you share it?

Arvantis: It was the same.

Jefferson: No?! Seriously?

Arvantis: Yes, seriously.

Jefferson: Oh...well...that is nice. Okay...so, in that lifetime, did you find out about me through the archives as well?

Arvantis: No.

Jefferson: How?

Arvantis: I was simply able to communicate to you directly.

Jefferson: Wow...

Arvantis: I had a knowing for some reason. It was part of my life to do that and to know that and to be aware of that. Just as I would know that there was daylight or if the Sun had set.

Jefferson: Wow...

Arvantis: It was simply a part of my awareness.

Jefferson: And close to the end of my life, what can you tell me about it?

Arvantis: Close to the end of your life when?

Jefferson: As Giordano Bruno.

Arvantis: You were then at a state of greater ease and comfort with the ability to be in the world of Earth and to have a sense of joy. To be more at ease with the society of humans. To not be as downtrodden in your attitude towards people in general. A greater sense of appreciation was present for you for life. You had more appreciation for others, other ideas, yourself, and life, compared to when you were younger.

Jefferson: Okay. Did I know before I was born as Giordano that I might die in that lifetime due to people with different religious beliefs burning me at the stake?

Arvantis: This was a choice that you had made before birth.

Jefferson: Because...?

Arvantis: You wanted to have that experience. There was something in there that excited you.

Jefferson: Right?!

Arvantis: You felt that way of transitioning out of the physical world was one way that might be most attractive to you. You had a couple of other choices that you set up before you were born, but as you moved on in your life that became the one you chose to experience. At times in your aware state while in that embodiment, you thought of it. There were things about it that you were consciously aware of that attracted you. You felt it might be a way to get people's attention. You felt it might be a way to get your work noticed. So you did have a bit of a plan set up around the idea. There were many people there to be a part of that and then to become more aware of what it was you had to share, information that was important for you to leave behind. Many people then became aware of it, read it, and learned to make their own choices in life as a result of the information you left.

Jefferson: And after I left that incarnation, did I go to your planet to thank you and give you a hug?

Arvantis: Yes.

Jefferson: I did?

Arvantis: You did!

Jefferson: Okay. Wow! So basically, one idea of that lifetime was to bring in new information and perhaps be an example that we all should speak our heart and never give up the truth in us no matter how threatening the attitudes are of people around us?

Arvantis: That would be part of the idea.

Jefferson: What was the main idea to leave that life that way?

Arvantis: Primarily to gather more people's attention to what it was you were saying. It was a bright light shining on the work that you had put together for then more people to see it, to be aware of it.

Jefferson: That's nice! It's one of the reasons I appreciate that lifetime so much. Now, let us explore a bit more your present world and how you guys deal with the idea of time. How have you in your world grown up to understand the idea of time?

Arvantis: Time allows me opportunity to have physical experiences of life growing, developing, changing. With the idea of time, I have made new discoveries since I was born, and I will make new discoveries in the future that are exciting for me as well. In a sense, time is like something I can look forward to and also look back at and experience what I have explored and discovered before. Experiences that seem to be of past, present, and future life are things that time affords me the opportunity to create.

Yes, "it is all here and now," but if I don't create the experience of a past, a present, and a future timeframe, then I am not able to experience any change and growth taking place. All of existence would be present to me in its full state of simultaneous beingness so nothing would change to me.

Having a sense of time allows me to experience change taking place in life over time, or moving forward, or making progress, or having people I can look forward to meeting tomorrow, or having mysterious and enjoyable moments present themselves to me in five minutes or five years from now. Without a sense of time in this way, I can't then look forward to meeting a dear friend tomorrow because I am already meeting them now. And I wouldn't be able to experience a child growing up because the child exists in all ages now.

Jefferson: Oh.

Arvantis: Time affords the opportunity to have a physical experience, change over time. Without time, physical experience would not possible. Physicality necessitates having the idea of time.

Jefferson: There are people on Earth that are focused on finding a way to stop aging. If you wanted to, could you stop aging?

Arvantis: Yes, it would be possible.

Jefferson: How would you do that?

Arvantis: I would simply stop the genetic codes, the concepts, the intentions that are considered genes that control the aging mechanism in my physiology.

Jefferson: So I can do that myself.

Arvantis: It is possible, but in your world it isn't very probable given the strength of energies around you that aren't willing to accept that it's possible. You are living there in that realm, swimming in those frequencies, and are somewhat influenced by the predominant choice of that collective conscious which chooses to believe that you can't do it.

Jefferson: I see.

Arvantis: So it is an option, possibly, but not likely for you to alter your genetic make up and remain alive in your physical form for an eternity. It is not likely that you would choose that.

Jefferson: What about if I stayed here for just...like...the span of time of two-hundred years and in that two-hundred years I still look the way I look today?

Arvantis: If that is your strongest desire and you choose that, it will occur for you.

Jefferson: Even though the collective consciousness is not going for that?

Arvantis: Yes, but remember that is part of your consciousness too, the collective consciousness.

Jefferson: Yes, right. Do you have Arkoreuns that are overweight?

Arvantis: No.

Jefferson: So that is not a choice that you guys make?

Arvantis: A choice to be overweight?

Jefferson: Yeah, that's not interesting for you?

Arvantis: Correct.

Jefferson: Would you say, in that sense, that everything is a choice?

Arvantis: Yes, in reference to what you are asking.

Jefferson: How is the weather on your planet? Does it rain?

Arvantis: We do have moisture. We do have rivers. We do have warmth, and Sun, and dryness as well. We do have what you would consider as a breeze. It doesn't get windy very strong. Maybe ten to fifteen of what you would consider miles per hours or knots of wind speed on your world. We don't then have hurricanes, or tornados, or typhoons, or tsunamis. We don't have large oceans as you have on your world. We do have some bodies of water but nothing of the size your world has. The weather is always in a climate range that we are very comfortable in. It doesn't get, what you might call, too hot or too cold. We don't have to seek shade. We don't have to seek warmth from the weather changing.

Jefferson: What is the average temperature?

Arvantis: It would be approximately 123 to 128 of your Fahrenheit.

Jefferson: Can you talk about fashions? Are your clothes like ours?

Arvantis: We do not have the same materials as yours. We do not have the variety of fashion in clothing that you have. We do not have the abundant decorative items sewn onto our clothes. We do have some artwork on the clothing and each person generally will do that theirself, add some form of art that they are attracted to, some imagery or symbolism that they will create using particular organic plant matters to make colors they can place on the fabric, on the clothing.

Jefferson: Are you wearing any clothing now?

Arvantis: Yes. I have a soft blue shirt on and some long, very lose fitting, what you might think of as pants.

Jefferson: And do you twalk barefoot?

Arvantis: Frequently yes. Our feet are very strong and the skin on the bottom of our feet is very think and capable of moving across a variety of protruding and sharp objects on some of the rock surfaces we might encounter in our travels by foot.

Jefferson: Wouldn't the existence of clothes create the need for a wardrobe?

Arvantis: There are some who have more then one clothing item but generally not. One is sufficient.

Jefferson: Well, don't you have to wash it? When it's dirty and you put it to wash, do you stay naked?

Arvantis: It tends to have an internal conscious ability to self cleanse its interacting with our body, with our skin. It is a relationship and so it doesn't, in that sense, become soiled by bodily oils or ground matter. It is able to, in a sense, remain its own molecular quality and state such that it doesn't take on the embodiments of other matter.

Jefferson: You said your houses don't have bathrooms. Does that mean that your physiology transforms everything you eat to the point where you don't have to do any trips to the toilet?

Arvantis: Yes. Very convenient.

Jefferson: Right! That's very convenient! Is that because you don't eat more than you need?

Arvantis: It is simply the way our bodies are designed to function. We have a form of elimination of cellular structures, and food items we may consume don't require the form of elimination you have in your bodies.

Jefferson: Okay.

Arvantis: There are some in your world that have attained this ability. Very few. And they eat quite a different diet then most of you are aware of or choose to consume.

Jefferson: Yeah, there are people that live on light!

Arvantis: It's similar to that, but not only that for we do interact with some of the forms of food on our world. Some of the plant matter is food for us on our world.

Jefferson: And seeds, as you spoke of before?

Arvantis: Yes.

Jefferson: Well, you also said there are no sinks in your houses. Does that mean you also don't have any mirrors and that you don't need to shave?

Arvantis: Yes.

Jefferson: Don't you get cavities if you don't brush your teeth?

Arvantis: No.

Jefferson: How many teeth does an adult have?

Arvantis: Twenty-two on the top and twenty-two on the bottom.

Jefferson: Is your tongue like ours?

Arvantis: It serves a similar function, but the shape, and the texture, and the skin is a little bit different than yours.

Jefferson: How so?

Arvantis: There is a bit more of a thickness to our tongue, a little bit more of a tactile structure to it that enables us then to touch the food with our tongue more effectively. It is as though it has little fingers, very minuscule fingers, on the surface of the tongue that are able to reach out and touch the foods that we might eat or even particular plants that we are simply tasting or exploring more of their nature by having contact with our tongues.

Jefferson: If there are no showers in your houses, when you need to get clean, do you lick yourselves like our cats do?

Arvantis: We do not do that, no. At times we can move out into the rivers, but again, our body tends to have a way of interacting with the environment thus that it doesn't need washing as you do on your world generally consider the idea of having to take a bath. We do at times enjoy being in, swimming in, the water in the river. That can change the texture and the energy of our surface skin matter, and it might seem a bit more clean to someone such as yourself, but that isn't what is occurring. It is simply a little bit of a different state of being as a result of interacting with the water.

Jefferson: When you get wet, don't you need towels to dry yourselves?

Arvantis: We could use a towel, but we don't. It isn't necessary. The water tends to bead off us fairly quickly. Certainly in a timing that is workable for us, comfortable for us.

Jefferson: When you swim, do you swim with your clothes on?

Arvantis: We may. Not always. Sometimes the clothes enjoy being in the water as well. So we all go for a swim together.

Jefferson: Oh, wow! Cats in my world don't like water, to my knowledge. It doesn't seem to be the same with you?

Arvantis: We do have a different physiology.

Jefferson: Oh, yes. Still on the subject of the Arkoreuns, do you guys have enough differences that would define when a person is a child, a teenager, an adult, and an elder?

Arvantis: We do.

Jefferson: What are the main differences from childhood to teenagerhood?

Arvantis: Generally the children and the infants require more care or attention, as in your world. The teenagers, what you would consider moving from a child into an adult state, tend to be very curious about many different things, not as focused on one idea as more adults tend to be. And the adults tend to oversee the community, to overlook the well-being and congruent ongoing harmony amongst the community as a whole.

Jefferson: And are the elders the teachers?

Arvantis: There are adults who are considered teachers.

Jefferson: And what are the elders for?

Arvantis: We don't really make a distinction between the adults and the elders.

Jefferson: What age is considered the childhood?

Arvantis: Generally in the ages of five to ten.

Jefferson: What age do you live the teenagerhood?

Arvantis: Generally in the ages of thirteen to nineteen.

Jefferson: Oh, so you're an adult pretty young. How do you know that someone is an adult? Do you have a graduation ceremony at some point?

Arvantis: We do not have any fine point of delineation. It is something that just occurs overtime.

Jefferson: Do you have an estimation of how many Arkoreuns are on your planet? On Earth we have almost seven billion humans.

Arvantis: We have approximately 300,000.

Jefferson: And do you extend your civilization onto the fourteen planets in your Solar System or does each planet have a different society on it?

Arvantis: We have two other planets with life forms. We visit, but we don't live on any of those planets on a regular basis.

Jefferson: Oh...the other planets that you visit, are they amongst the fourteen?

Arvantis: Yes, they are.

Jefferson: Are the life forms there similar to yours?

Arvantis: They do have quite a few similarities, yes.

Jefferson: They are different civilizations?

Arvantis: They are distinctly different, but they operate similar to us in many respects.

Jefferson: Okay.

Arvantis: Their worlds are, like ours, small in number compared to the seven- billion on your world. There are approximately 400,000 and 500,000 on each of the other two inhabited planets.

Jefferson: And...

Arvantis: They are not feline as we are.

Jefferson: They are not?

Arvantis: They are not canine either so we get along very well. Not that we do not get along with "the dogs" from Sirius. They are lovely as well!

Jefferson: Oh. So there are dogs on Sirius?

Just a play on words around the idea of the "dog star" of Sirius.

Jefferson: Oh, okay. What are those two races?

Arvantis: They are the Arailians and the Roombah

Jefferson: And I am still not sure if I understood, are they felinoid, reptilian, pleiadian...what are they?

Arvantis: They are somewhat human, but they don't all have two legs. Some have four-leg physiology to them.

Jefferson: And on your planet, do you have a government or a

monetary system?

Arvantis: We do not, nor do they!

Jefferson: How do you work out order and progress as a society?

Arvantis: By not creating disorder in our society.

Jefferson: How do you grow spiritually? How do you work out your spiritual evolution? Do you go to church?

Arvantis: We do not have such an institution. We follow our heart. We do what is of greatest sensing for us to do. That then is what would be most joyful for us to do.

Jefferson: How do you develop your physical strength if you don't do sports? Do you go to the gym?

Arvantis: We have all the strength we need just by following and doing what it is of greatest joy for us to do. Our genetic structure always supports this form of existence for us. Our genetic structure is a form of consciousness that has awareness on levels of awareness that we don't need to be aware of. It makes it easier for us to simply "kick back" and enjoy the life we have created for ourselves here. We don't have to monitor all of the variables in life. Out genes do that form of monitoring, that form of interacting, and calculating, and adjusting, and overseeing of the physiological interactions in our embodiment within our physical world. Does that answer your question?

Jefferson: It does! Do you have the same number of chakras as we do?

Arvantis: No.

Jefferson: How many chakras do you have?

Arvantis: We have a multitude of chakras in our primary spinal region. We have one at the bottom of the spine, one at the top of our skull and we have one at the heart region. They are very strong, and they create a tubular chakra that then flows to the rest of the spinal region of our torso and neck and our skull region. Our feet, and our hands, and our knees also have what could be considered chakras, very powerful such that they then create a tubular chakra into the heart region, into the chakra of the heart region. It is more of a tubular chakra idea.

Jefferson: What are the chakras for?

Arvantis: They are a form of gateway that interacts with the subtle realms of existence, and they bring forth inner energies, and understandings, and consciousnesses from the subtle realms into our physical form. They are like a gate in which the translation from the subtle realm into our physical realm can take place. They are the adjusters. They are the frequency adjusters from the subtle to the physical and also from our physical back out to the subtle realms. Do you follow that idea?

Jefferson: I do. It seems that this works the same way with us.

Arvantis: Yes it does.

Jefferson: It's just that we are not fully aware of that.

Arvantis: And your chakras are a little bit different in location as well in how they form and interact with one another?

Jefferson: Do you have an idea why you have less then we have?

Arvantis: Simply for us to have the type of experience we've chosen to have on this planet. It's a different area, a different frequency. It requires a different physiological make up and structure. So it then thus is compatible for this physical frequency of reality. It works perfectly here.

Jefferson: I see. Do you have people that get hurt and need healers?

Arvantis: Not as you experience hurt, physiologically. There can at times be something that will cause a wound and then we have those present, whoever is there with that person, to be like healers with that person. They group their minds, and energy, and hearts, and feelings together to bring about healing, a returning back to the state of being before the wound was created.

Jefferson: Oh, I see. So it's more of an energetic invitation for that which makes matter to go back to the prior healthy state?

Arvantis: We work as a team to heal a wound. It could be called the prior state but it is simply back to the state of what we experience as a whole body without the wound. It is not the same state; it just appears to be a prior similar state. Not the same, but similar.

Jefferson: You said you could go long distances at high speed without getting tired.

Arvantis: Yes.

Jefferson: And I asked you what other means of transports you have but then I interrupted you...so...other then spacecrafts, can you give us an idea of what other means of transport you have at this time?

Arvantis: We do travel along the rivers at times. We have what could be considered a boat. A floatation canoe of sorts, a kayak of sorts, and there are oars that we work with.

Jefferson: Do you go up in trees really high and jump branch to branch through the trees to get to other places as well?

Arvantis: We don't usually swing around in trees like you might see monkeys in your world doing, but we do at times go up into the trees and we can climb around quite effectively and agilely. We do enjoy that type of activity!

Jefferson: And do your nails extend to grasp the tree branches?

Arvantis: We do not claw the trees. We have nails of a sort, similar to yours, but we do not get sharp and pointy nails that we would use like talons of an eagle, or a bird, or a cat in your world.

Jefferson: Okay, well. There is one more question that I want to ask.

Arvantis: Yes.

Jefferson: Do Arkoreuns enjoy what we would call dating?

Arvantis: We have interactions together. Yes!

Jefferson: And do your women have the experience of what we would consider pregnancy?

Arvantis: Yes.

Jefferson: And, does it happen the same way it happens on Earth?

Arvantis: It is similar. The timeframe can be shorter or longer.

Jefferson: Do the men and woman have reproductive anatomy similar to ours?

Arvantis: This is similar.

Jefferson: Okay. Do you have an age where Arkoreun men are more interested in women and women are more interested in men?

Arvantis: That is around nine to twelve year range where that begins to develop more fully and that attraction begins to bond with more strength.

Jefferson: And then do you end up getting married?

Arvantis: No! Not as you have an institution of marriage.

Jefferson: But...do you get together with a person for the entire life?

Arvantis: This does occur. Yes!

Jefferson: But it's not...necessarily...

Arvantis: It doesn't always.

Jefferson: And do you have a girlfriend?

Arvantis: I at present have one.

Jefferson: But you are not married?

Arvantis: I am presently "married".

Jefferson: You are?

Arvantis: But not in the terms of what you consider marriage.

Jefferson: In what terms are you married?

Arvantis: That we interact with each other and don't interact with others, by choice. In the form that you might consider two people in an intimate physical relationship with one another.

Jefferson: Oh I see...and...do you have children?

Arvantis: I do not. Nor does she from any other prior interaction with another.

Jefferson: She is younger than you?

Arvantis: She is. Yes.

Jefferson: How old is she?

Arvantis: Approximately twenty-four of —

Jefferson: That is half your age!

Arvantis: — of what you would consider twenty-four. Not on my world. She is approximately twenty-four on your world.

Jefferson: And on my world, how old are you?

Arvantis: I am approximately twenty five on your world.

Jefferson: Okay, that makes sense. Do you have any parting thoughts you would like to share with me?

Arvantis: I will again express our, and my, joy to have had this interaction with you, and for your curiosity in our world, and that we may become in this way more familiar for you, more like fellow humans that you are willing and able to interact with easily, comfortably, and excitingly, and be looking forward to meeting us in person.

Jefferson: Yes!

Arvantis: To share and write more details of who it is that we are so you can have a sense of what this is and who we are more clearly. So that the ideas you may have had of us as being "alien creatures" is cleared away and with it any sense of being frightened by ideas of us. In time, when you think of us, you will thus be able to think of us as friends and as family.

Jefferson: Nice...well, I thank you very much for all that you are doing in bringing all these ideas from your world. It is really exciting for me personally because you are my future self!

Yes! Oh, joyful! Wonderful! Yeeeees!

Jefferson: Well, very well. Thank you very much, and I will talk to you soon!

Arvantis: We look forward to that timing together. Much joy be it in the step with you. Joy in every step you take! We will be with you another way, another time. Until then, here we are and here we go!

Jefferson: Thank you

Chapter 3

Extraterrestrial Dragons and Earth Spacecrafts

"It is a great joy for us that you move forward in this way with greater willingness to define us as a reality, to give us greater credence, more sense of validity, and thus then in doing so you are putting that out and therefore you get back greater opportunities, frequencies, to experience us in more real ways."

- Arvantis

December 29th, 2009

Arvantis: Most wonderful to be here with you in this "how are you" moment together.

Jefferson: It is lovely to speak to you!

Arvantis: Yes, very good indeed to have this time to communicate in this format. Vocal to vocal contact. Communicating clearly, concisely, from one word, one thought, one sharing after another. One to the next, yes. Lovely to interact with you in this way. How are you moving in this moment and in what direction would you like to go?

Jefferson: I would like to ask you something "off the record."

Arvantis: Off the record...didn't realize we were standing on one.

Jefferson: Have I personally met a star visitor?

Arvantis: You have many visitors that are stars, yes, what do you mean by star visitor? Explain.

Jefferson: Extraterrestrial beings, that would—

Arvantis: Yes, that is what I am, and I am visiting with you now. So could you be more clear in the question?

Jefferson: Physically!

Arvantis: That occurs, but you are not always awake when it happens. So perhaps you don't remember.

Jefferson: Who visited me?

Arvantis: I have, occasionally, but more often then not you have some visitors that are of your own parallel race like a Zeta, like a Grey. But they are you on a slightly different reality, a slightly different frequency.

Jefferson: Oh my! So…so…basically you're saying that I have in this lifetime been physically visited by a Zeta.

Arvantis: Yes.

Jefferson: And that Zeta is an incarnation of myself in that race?

Arvantis: Yes.

Jefferson: Wow…and when was the last time that happened?

Arvantis: About three months ago?

Jefferson: Can they walk through walls or do they have to open the door and everything?

Arvantis: They can simply adjust their frequency.

Jefferson: Wow...oh my. And what was the reason of the visit?

Arvantis: Just to say hello! Make a few adjustments to your physiology. Let you talk about some things that were interesting to you that were of a curious nature for you. Get a few ideas. Ask a few questions. Kind of like what you're doing now other than the physiological adjustments to some of your bodily beingness.

Jefferson: And how long was that visit?

Arvantis: Approximately two-and-a-half hours of your timing. Took an instant in ours!

Jefferson: And how come I don't remember anything?

Arvantis: It is something that doesn't suit your current aware state of being, the life you are living. It doesn't really apply in a way that would be most supportive to what you want to experience here in your present aware state, your present life.

Jefferson: Wow...and when was the last time you visited me?

Arvantis: Oh, it's been about three-and-a-half months.

Jefferson: And how did you get here?

Arvantis: I was part of a receivership, a program where several of us came together and, in a sense, arrived here in a particular portal of frequency. It's sort of like a time travel, moving from one sound-frequency of reality to that one where you were.

Jefferson: Okay.

Arvantis: There were others who made other stops along the way to see other people, as it were. And I was visiting then with you when it was my stop, as though the bus stopped at your residence and I got out for a visit.

Jefferson: And around what time was that?

Arvantis: It was midnight.

Jefferson: And I received you?

Arvantis: Well, that receivership has to do with the idea of several of us from different races getting together in a craft and coming down and making stops to visit other people, other humans incarnated in your life on your planet presently. So the idea then is not that you received me but you did have contact with me in that way, communication, yes.

Jefferson: Wow. So you have already been physically on Earth?

Arvantis: Yes!

Jefferson: Oh my...that's exciting! And...what happened when you came and visited me?

Arvantis: We had a brief visit just to let you know that things were going to start accelerating, in a sense, things were going to begin to blossom in your connection with me. And that we would begin having more spoken dialogue in a more aware state for you such as this that is now occurring.

Jefferson: What state of consciousness was I...because I don't remember!

Arvantis: You were awake as you are now, however, it is a memory, in a sense, that isn't accessed by your present state of awareness for reasons of your own choosing.

Jefferson: Wow.... that is so exciting! And were you wearing clothes?

Arvantis: Yes.

Jefferson: And you had the blue shirt?

Arvantis: Well, we had our appropriate attire for the visitation.

Jefferson: Yeah...can you breathe in our atmosphere?

Arvantis: I was able to, yes.

Jefferson: Wow, okay, so, obviously you got prepared before you came.

Arvantis: There are some adjustments I make.

Jefferson: And did you visit me before those three years?

Arvantis: Three-and-a-half months.

Jefferson: Oh yes, sorry, I meant months. Three-and-a-half months, yeah. Did you visit me before that?

Arvantis: I have.

Jefferson: How many times?

Arvantis: Approximately twelve.

Jefferson: Okay. Wow! And people who get such a visitation, if they go under hypnosis, they will be able to recall what happened, right?

Arvantis: Sometimes not...sometimes yes!

Jefferson: Okay. And after the last time you've been here, what happened once you arrived back home? I imagine that as you returned to your planet, people would start asking questions about how the visit was, right?

Arvantis: I had a briefing with some of those on my world just to let them know how it went, yes. They shared their input, as it were, offered suggestions and insights. They have, in a sense, become experts in this type of briefing, and they have much to offer to me so the next time I can be more skilled at the conversation and interaction when we meet.

Jefferson: And can you tell something about the briefing? The last

briefing that you had, how was it, what came up that was interesting for you?

Arvantis: They wanted to know why you were moving out of the bay area of San Francisco, California. I explained to them you felt there was no forward momentum in the direction of your greatest joy, to be held in the career, workplace there. And that you would move where you had the opportunity to be roofed, housed, and have more free time to follow what you prefer to do.

Jefferson: Yes!

Arvantis: Which they understood and they offered some insights that I may share next meeting with you if that occurs before you move. It may, it may not. We shall see. I am not in a position to say either way at this timing.

Jefferson: Sure. And how do these meetings assist and support me, us, if we don't remember them?

Arvantis: You do remember enough to function and move forward and take the steps that will be most sensorially exciting for you and attract new opportunities into your life so you can choose the ones that will keep you on the path that is of greatest joy for you. You have a new frequency as result of such meetings that then will attract you to the new opportunities more easily. It is like a frequency adjustment that occurs so that what you put out will be more in alignment with what you truly prefer to be getting back in your life. The opportunities that come to you will be more in alignment with the new frequency you have adjusted to and are now "putting out," while prior frequencies would not necessarily have been most optimum in attracting the new opportunities to you if you had not had the frequency adjustment.

The adjustment can simply be a word, a sound, a dialogue, a lot of talking, a feeling, a sensorial emotion, or any combination of these. They can make for a frequency adjustment, but it is always with your acceptance, choice, willingness, understanding, and cooperation that such a frequency adjustment would occur.

Jefferson: And the last time we met was brief. How long was it?

Arvantis: In your time, approximately two hours. For us it was an instant! But again, the idea in terms of the timeframe you are asking that is most relevant to the question as you ask it is, two hours of your time.

Jefferson: Sure…okay. That was the question I had that was "off the record." So now—

Arvantis: Time to get back on the record?

Jefferson: Yes.

Arvantis: Get spinning around?

Jefferson: So…oh my gosh…there are so many things going on. I had no idea that this happened…or perhaps I had? Anyway, let's move in this direction now. We usually set up these encounters with you through the channeler Shaun without considering what time it can be in your world. Maybe we are waking you up in the middle of your night without knowing. Is that the case today?

Arvantis: Yes! I was having a lovely dream. Why are you coming here and knocking on my door at this hour and waking me up!

Jefferson: No, seriously, what time is it there?

Arvantis: We had a bit of a sunrise, approximately half-hour ago.

Jefferson: Oh.

Arvantis: There is a brilliant and lovely bright new day that is lighting up our sky overhead for us to partake in and enjoy ever so wonderfully. We appreciate this experience and co-creation with our planet and Sun as it shines and brings forth a new day rising forth within our aware states to play.

Jefferson: Is your planet, 7.5 times smaller than Earth or does it rotate around your Sun 7.5 times quicker?

Arvantis: On average, approximately three times faster than yours.

Jefferson: How do you count time?

Arvantis: We are relating the idea of revolutions around our Sun. Similar to how you do in this discussion with you of time.

Jefferson: Do you work with the idea of minutes, hours, days, weeks, month, and then years?

Arvantis: We are familiar with the idea of particular orbits that our planet makes around the Sun of our solar system. It could be like one orbit, one revolution, in that sense, but we don't keep track of the hours, and the minutes, and the seconds as you do.

Jefferson: Oh, I see.

Arvantis: We understand that when we are in a particular region of our yearly orbit there will be variations in the atmosphere, as you have on your world seasons, so we are aware of that as reference to time as well. You have the idea of summertime, and springtime, and wintertime and we have a sense of time in that respect too.

Jefferson: How long is an entire year for you?

Arvantis: That would be one revolution of our planet's movement around our Sun.

Jefferson: Oh, okay. So what we call a year, you would call one revolution?

Arvantis: Well, you could call your year a revolution.

Jefferson: Right!?

Arvantis: If you want to.

Jefferson: So if I was to ask you what day is today, what would you answer?

Arvantis: It is the day before tomorrow. We don't have a calendar set up the way you do.

Jefferson: Oh...

Arvantis: We don't separate the ideas the way you do! Monday, Tuesday, Wednesday, Thursday and so on.

Jefferson: Before I—

Arvantis: Imagine if you could for a moment, what would be different in your world if you threw out the calendar. Not that we are suggesting to do that. Just imagine what that life would be like not to have hours, minutes, and seconds. Not to have a Monday and Tuesday and so on. How might things change for you if all were doing that as well? How might your world and society change? Not that we are suggesting you do that. Just imagine it. Perhaps when you have some time on your own. Play with the idea. Get a sense of what that might feel like and you will get to have a little bit more of the idea of what it is like for us in terms of how we experience *time* on our world.

Jefferson: I have been doing that for a while, and it's really cool. I enjoy it when I can. It is indeed something. But so many people have to work in places where keeping track of time is so important. Yet, a person must be following their excitement, otherwise it's boring.

Arvantis: What is boring?

Jefferson: For example, when I am doing something that I don't like — so I am not following my heart's excitement — I look over at the clock and it seems to just be standing still.

Arvantis: Why would you do such a thing?

Jefferson: I know, right!? It doesn't make sense! So that's why I retired myself from the clock idea. I don't consult the calendar if I can. I just do what I can, and I trust that the best is going to happen. You know, that is it!

Arvantis: What do you trust in?

Jefferson: I trust in the Universe and the laws of the Universe. I think I understand them a little bit. I have fun today. I have fun tomorrow. I am responsible to others, and I stay within integrity, and I keep following my highest excitement and then things seem to "fall from the skies!"

Arvantis: What's falling?

Jefferson: **Abundance!**

Arvantis: All right.

Jefferson: **Yeah.**

Arvantis: Abundance of what?

Jefferson: **Abundance of more excitement and more reasons to continue moving through the present days.**

Arvantis: Very well.

Jefferson: **Very well it is! So I was going to ask you this, would you say that our automobiles, our trains, our planes, are all things that are extensions of the level of awareness of our consciousness...that consciousness has created to live within?**

Arvantis: You could look at it that way.

Jefferson: **In your sensing, do you see us evolving to a place where we are going to have spaceships like yours?**

Arvantis: You are moving to a place now as a collective, the momentum is growing and is very strong, suggesting that you will arrive at that place. They will not be metal crafts for much longer. There are various types of materials that will be used to produce a craft, a spacecraft, that will be quite different than anything you presently have in your popular public awareness.

Jefferson: **Talking about craft, is it possible that a human being can visit another planet and come back and not know that he did so?**

Arvantis: Yes! Just as I can meet you and you don't remember that. You don't recall having that interaction.

Jefferson: Yeah, but you are from a more evolved race and you can visit other planets! Humans would have to be "taken!"

Arvantis: They "choose" to go for the ride.

Jefferson: Yeah.

Arvantis: They aren't "taken" against their will.

Jefferson: I know, I know, going for a ride is actually what I meant. Have I been to any other planets in this lifetime?

Arvantis: You have been to approximately four.

Jefferson: No, I mean physically?

Arvantis: Yes.

Jefferson: Four planets. Have I been to yours?

Arvantis: That is something that will occur in the future, as you consider time.

Jefferson: Then what planets have I visited?

Arvantis: You were on the planet of your Jupiter. You had a space suit and something that was like an enormous spacecraft that could handle the atmosphere. This Jupiter was at a slightly different frequency than what you currently observe Jupiter to be in your night sky. It was a slightly different dimension of reality. So it wasn't like you were just standing on its surface like you are standing on Earth today. You had space suit like equipment and a craft around you, and there were others present who were at the helm of the visit there.

Jefferson: So this is one of the planets that I have visited physically in this lifetime.

Arvantis: One of the four.

Jefferson: Yeah. Jupiter…and when was that?

Arvantis: You were nine!

Jefferson: Nine? How did I get there?

Arvantis: We took you! You wanted to visit a planet and that was what you were most excited about and there was opportunity to go there in the alignments of energies so we were able to move forth in that journey.

Jefferson: How long does a journey like that take?

Arvantis: A blink-of-an-eye.

Jefferson: Yeah for you, but for us?

Arvantis: It is the same.

Jefferson: No…you know…we work with time so there are seconds, and then minutes, and then hours.

Arvantis: Well, if we were to work on that time frame, you wouldn't have even arrived yet. If you moved at the speed of your current crafts.

Jefferson: Oh true. So…okay, and what was the second planet I visited.

Arvantis: There was the planet Helios in a region of the Sirius space section. That was something you were able to walk around on, similar to how you do on Earth. You had a breathing apparatus to assist with some variations in the type of oxygen on that surface of Helios.

Jefferson: And…what age was I?

Arvantis: Nine.

Jefferson: Wow, I was quite outgoing huh?

Arvantis: It was part of the same trip when you were on Jupiter.

Jefferson: Oh, it was the same trip. And what was the other planet?

Arvantis: There was an opportunity to visit a planet in the Orion Belt, as you look at your night sky. The planet was in the Orion Belt region. The name isn't something that will come forth at the present timing.

Jefferson: And was it the same travel?

Arvantis: It was.

Jefferson: And the other one?

Arvantis: The other one was in a region of your Arcturus.

Jefferson: And it was the same trip?

Arvantis: That was approximately three years later when you were twelve!

Jefferson: And how did that happen?

Arvantis: We had an opportunity to take you there for some renewal of your physiology. Some friction was occurring in your family, and it was not very soothing for you so we took you on a bit of a holiday, a vacation.

On Arcturus there were some very soothing energies. They were very calibrating for you in a way that allowed you to come back and feel more at home amongst the friction that was occurring in the family and some of the relatives that you were living with at that time.

Jefferson: Did you call me somehow and say, "I'm going to come pick you up so get ready?"

Arvantis: In a matter of speaking, but it wasn't something you would have been aware of in the way that you are aware of this conversation now. Your awareness exists on many levels.

Jefferson: Sure. How did I enter the craft?

Arvantis: We brought you up. A form of vibrational attunement. Your body is, in a sense, encapsulated by a particular frequency of light energy and then the adjustment on your vibration is calibrated and then you are brought forward and aboard the craft. And there you are before us, on board.

Jefferson: And what does that craft look like?

Arvantis: It's a bit of a round sphere with some triangular protrusions from the surface of the round sphere, three to five triangular protrusions that have four sides – somewhat like pyramids in your Egypt region. The triangular protrusions do change shape, color, and size, as we move through frequencies from one place to another.

Jefferson: Are these visitations dangerous for you?

Arvantis: There is no danger. There is great joy, and fun, and excitement.

Jefferson: Even though there is the risk that someone could see you?

Arvantis: That would not be done in a way that would be of danger as you referred to the idea of danger.

Jefferson: Thank you for sharing that! Now, share with me some ideas about the spaceship of your planet. Does it need a pilot?

Arvantis: There are pilots. There is someone guiding, yes. Very tuned in to the craft that is conscious. It has a form of life force within its own structure and there is someone then that tunes to that consciousness that is able to guide it and give it information as to where the person or the people would like to go.

Jefferson: I see.

Arvantis: And that then is a form of piloting. They aren't at a control wheel with lots of tiny instrument panels and gauges. That isn't something we are, as a pilot, needing to observe and to understand. Our craft don't function with all that type of detailed instrumentation that you would find on many of your craft.

Jefferson: Do you need to study how to pilot it?

Arvantis: There is a little bit of learning that takes place but not to the degree that you find on your world to become a pilot of a plane.

Jefferson: Has anybody ever died in a plane accident?

Arvantis: Not in our world. We understand there are some extraterrestrial races where that can occur and has, in our understanding. We don't function in that particular level of craftsmanship.

Jefferson: What is the main difference then?

Arvantis: The conscious state of awareness and creatorship of physical reality and that is the main difference. We create from a different frequency of consciousness, which will afford us then to create different types of space travel and spacecrafts from which to travel with.

Jefferson: Can a person possess a spacecraft?

Arvantis: Possess?

Jefferson: Yeah.

Arvantis: Own?

Jefferson: Yes.

Arvantis: We don't have ownership, in that sense. But a craft can be more keyed to the consciousness of one particular person. That can occur.

Jefferson: Hmm.

Arvantis: Much like you have people there who tend to interact with you, like friends. You don't really own them but you are able to relate to them and you have rapport. You get along with them. You have a friendship, a bonding, a relationship energetically, in that sense. But there is no ownership in the relationship.

Jefferson: In your visits to Earth, has anybody of your family ever come with you?

Arvantis: Has anybody visited with me?

Jefferson: Yes.

Arvantis: Yes, in the receiverships we have several extraterrestrials who are aboard that will stop over in different locations and meet with people such as when I stop over your location to meet with you.

Jefferson: And has anybody from your immediate family come...like your brother, or your sister, or your mom?

Arvantis: I have not had that. No!

Jefferson: Okay. I was wondering as we are talking about family...how old is your family in Earth years...like your younger brother, how old is he?

Arvantis: Approximately twelve.

Jefferson: And your oldest sister?

Arvantis: Approximately forty-eight.

Jefferson: On Earth, right?

Arvantis: Yes, translated to your time.

Jefferson: And your other sister?

Arvantis: Ninety on our world, about thirty on yours.

Jefferson: And the other one?

Arvantis: Ninety.

Jefferson: Oh...wait...your older sister...you have three older sisters. You are about twenty-five in Earth years. Your oldest sister is about forty-eight. The other is about thirty in Earth years, and the other one?

Arvantis: Yes, my younger brother is twelve.

Jefferson: Oh...your...both your older sisters are ninety on your world?

Arvantis: Yes!

Jefferson: Oh, they are twins?!

Arvantis: Yes!

Jefferson: That must be fun! Okay. Now...a human on Earth will often interact with a particular type of animal or pet through the course of their lifetime. I have interacted mostly with cats, dogs, and a parrot. A talking bird. How about you? Can you tell me what three animals you have interacted with on your planet?

Arvantis: We have large, like a cat, but it doesn't have claws and sharp teeth and it purrs very loudly. It can be the size of us but they tend to be smaller, half our size. The large ones might be similar in size to the lions and tigers on your world, but these are very friendly. They don't have sharp claws. They don't have sharp teeth. They don't have the same type of voracious characteristics that those on your world do. They don't feed off of other animals for survival. They are very much in tune with the idea of living off the nutrients, nourishmnets, somewhat like vegetable and plant like matter.

Jefferson: Hmm.

Arvantis: The foliage on the planet. Their teeth are very flat for chewing.

Jefferson: Do they look like a tiger or...what do they look like?

Arvantis: They have more of a greenish blue quality and color.

Jefferson: Okay.

Arvantis: They don't have the tiger stripes.

Jefferson: Yeah.

Arvantis: There is some variation in colors. Occasionally there are some with spots, some patches, but they aren't predominant on the surface of the skin that tends to be furry, a very soft and short fur that is very flexible, almost like velvet on your planet.

Jefferson: Oh, nice. If I were to go there, would they allow me to hop on like a horse?

Arvantis: No riding pets, no riding cats, no riding people on our world. But you can ask them if you want.

Jefferson: Can you talk to them?
They like people rides! Perhaps you could give them piggyback rides.

Jefferson: Yeah.

Arvantis: We don't have conversations with them as I have with you now.

Jefferson: No? Oh, okay.

But there is relationship. They do understand. They have sensing of where we are at during any given time and we with them as well. So there is some relationship, some communication that takes place. There is a friendly rapport, a bonding that exists.

Jefferson: What do they do for you?

Arvantis: They enrich our life. They share in the world together with us. They go about their day as they desire and their activities can contribute to upliftment in our experience of life.

Jefferson: Are they playful?

Arvantis: They are.

Jefferson: Tell me another animal other than that one that you interact with.

Arvantis: There are some that live in the trees. They are very…how you say, soft-spoken. Very tender hearted. A bit like a Koala Bear in your world. They don't come out to play, but if we are in their area and see them, they are welcoming of our willingness to interact with them. They don't talk as I talk to you now, but we engage in a form of interaction with them. They move slowly, but they are very strong and agile creatures. They are very powerful and about one-third the size of the cats that we were talking about before.

Jefferson: Sure.

Arvantis: There are quite a few of them. They tend to come out when the Sun is not at its high point. Generally in the mornings and in the evenings is when we are likely to see them. They tend to remain in heavy shaded areas through most of the afternoon.

Jefferson: And do you have what we would name a firefly?

Arvantis: There are not fireflies.

Jefferson: No? Anything similar?

Arvantis: We don't have fireflies! We do have some flowers that glow in the dark, not that the flower itself does, but—

Jefferson: The pigments!

Arvantis: There is some pigment on them, yes!

Jefferson: Yeah, I remember. Now, can you name another animal? I am kind of curious. It's enjoyable to hear that!

Arvantis: We have, like a bird, a variety. They tend to have more rounded head shapes.

Jefferson: Oh, like the owl.

Arvantis: More similar to that. They tend to fly around late in the evening, but they don't come out at night.

Jefferson: Oh.

Arvantis: We will see them occasionally in the day. They come in a variety of colors and sizes and they rarely get larger than the doves that you have on your world.

Jefferson: I see.

Arvantis: Some can be a little bit smaller, and they don't usually chirp. They do more like a humming sound, and there are no loud cawing birds like you have on your world. At times they seem to sing a hum back and forth together within their own species and sometimes between different species they will hum. It is very clear that they are humming together and responding to one another and creating a melody, communicating in various ways for various reasons. We aren't clear as to what they are saying. We can hypothesize as to what they might be saying or communicating, but we don't have a clear understanding of what they are communicating to one another. It's enjoyable to listen to them play their hums together and individually.

Jefferson: And what size is the biggest animal that can fly?

Arvantis: That would be it.

Jefferson: Oh, you don't have a dragon?

Arvantis: We don't have that.

Jefferson: Ah.

Arvantis: We don't have any creatures that come flying through the skies that would be bigger than a large dove on your world.

Jefferson: Oh, okay.

Arvantis: Not to say that we couldn't have some visit us.

Jefferson: Seriously? Have you ever had a dragon visiting you?

Arvantis: We have extraterrestrials that are what you might think of as dragons, but they don't reside on our planet. That would be more to visit. They don't breath fiery flames.

Jefferson: And they come down and they speak to you like...normal?

Arvantis: It is a form of telepathic communication that can occur.

Jefferson: And they look like dragons?

Arvantis: They look like a very friendly, soft dragon. Not like a sharp, pointy ominous creature, that is often how dragons in your world are presented.

Jefferson: And how big are they?

Arvantis: They can reach approximately twelve-foot wingspan and stand in the neighborhood of five to seven feet.

Jefferson: Can we ride on them?

Arvantis: This is not something we do.

Jefferson: You could ask them, right?

Arvantis: This is something we sense they would not want to do.

Jefferson: Oh, okay. Sorry guys! Hopefully they are not hearing.

Arvantis: They have no issue with the idea of asking about this.

Jefferson: Are they part of the Association of Worlds?

Arvantis: There are some, yes.

Jefferson: Can you travel to other planets without being granted permission?

Arvantis: We would not do that.

Jefferson: How does that permission work? You radio them or you call them?

Arvantis: There is a connection network that exists in the Association. We can go that route and the type of communication needed to get in touch with any particular race of extraterrestrials is, in a sense, translated through the Association. We can also use our own communication routes and send out telepathic suggestions to those we might want to contact, to ask if we could visit, and then will receive a response. If the response is something we don't understand, then that is generally a sign that it isn't the time to move further with that idea.

Jefferson: If you go through the Association, is there an office that you send a letter to or a number you call, how does it work? For example, you have two planets in your solar system that are inhabited. So say you want to go to one of those two planets and they don't know yet because you just had the idea. How do you communicate that to them?

Arvantis: It's a little bit like the way you are talking now, but with the telepathic connection. We will allow them to respond after we send out our wish or desire to communicate with them. If they are listening to that frequency, then they will respond and we then have a link up or a conversation with them. So it's very similar to the conversation we are having now, although it occurs telepathically, and since you don't really communicate telepathically it might seem like there's a missing link. You might ask, "How do you make the actual contact?" As you develop telepathic communication, you will begin to see that it really isn't all that different from when you walk in a room and there is someone else standing there and you just start talking to them. They are able to hear and respond to you. It begins to be more like that as you develop the telepathic link up within your own communicative abilities.

Jefferson: The first day that we communicated you said that you were going to celebrate for quite a few days.

Arvantis: That was quite enjoyable, yes! Thank you for reminding us, in that sense.

Jefferson: Since we had already met before, what was so new about this for you that it deserved such a celebration?

Arvantis: For us it was an opportunity to express our appreciation for your choice to be aware in this way that you now are.

Jefferson: Oh, cool! And when you celebrate, how do you do the celebration, what happens?

Arvantis: We relax outside in nature and give appreciation for it and for others, for one another and for you, for those interacting with you, and then that appreciation we send out is like a very colorful fourth of July firework streaming up into the night sky and expanding out suddenly into a variety of shapes, and colors, and designs of energy. This appreciation in consciousness then gradually glides back down to the surface of our awareness and to the surface of yours in this analogy of a firework.

We are then able to feel that energy coming back that we had sent out, that colorful design that we sent out comes back to us in a variety of different ways. Part of that is a response from you and those interacting with you. Then the celebration continues as we send out a response to what we get back from you and those interacting with you. It's like we send out another firework filled with the conscious awareness of appreciation, and understanding, and gratitude for what is taking place in our ability to co-create this experience together with you in this timing of our life.

We relax and take it all in, sending out appreciation in various ways with thoughts, feelings, ideas, and allowing those types of colors to move out and then come back to us after they have waved through your beingness on some level of your existence and you respond back to us in some way. Waves of appreciation going back and forth. Colorful designs of consciousness moving out and coming back in our celebration as we sit softly together and enjoy our creations, our co-creations together.

Jefferson: In this particular celebration, have I responded back to you?

Arvantis: You have!

Jefferson: How have I done that?

Arvantis: At times, with your conscious awareness. At other times, you do so energetically, vibrationally, colorationally, on other levels of your awareness. You will respond automatically without being aware of doing so. This is similar to how your autonomic nervous system can function – your heart beats and your eyes blink without you really thinking about it or being aware of it happening. It just occurs. It is part of the nature of your physiology and your subtle-energetic bodily being.

Jefferson: And as you receive my response, does the energy that I send take any shape or form? You said there is some coloration but does it take any shape or form?

Arvantis: There are, yes. More of a soft pattern of firework. Funworks moving forth from you, if you will, funworks instead of fireworks. Energies and colors in various sizes and shapes moving forth from you, moving out for us to respond to, to take in, to see, to feel, to experience, to be a part of that together.

Jefferson: Wow! Okay, now we are coming to the end our encounter today. Who is there with you today?

Arvantis: My younger brother.

Jefferson: What is his name?

Arvantis: Orse

Jefferson: How do you spell that?

Arvantis: O, r, s, e.

Jefferson: Orse. Hmm, alright. Ask him if he has any question for me.

Arvantis: One moment. {...*a brief moment of silence...*} When are you going to have that fixture replaced?

Jefferson: When am I going to have that what?!

Arvantis: Fixture.

Jefferson: What is that?

Arvantis: One moment. {...*a brief moment of silence...*} There are a few items in your vocabulary that are fixed. That you are, in a sense, fixated on. And he's asking, when are you going to have those fixtures replaced. So then there is the analogy if you were in your house, lets say you are in your kitchen and the light fixture, the glass that surrounds the light bulb, had been cracked or was chipped or was of a style simply that no longer suited you, you would go get a different light fixture of a different style, a different texture, a different design, a different presentation.

So there are a couple of words in your vocabulary that he is suggesting are like an old outdated fixture that don't really suit you, it is of a different design. It's an old model, if you will. He's not suggesting there is anything wrong with that; it's just that you could update it. You could go out and get a new, modern, more futuristic "fixture of vocabulary." So he's referring to a word or two that you are fixated on that comes out for you frequently and I understand he isn't going to tell you what it is. He's going to leave it up to you to see the fixture overhead, in your head, and decide if and when you want to change it. Not that you have to. He just wants to know if you are going to.

And really, it's his way of bringing something to your attention. That is part of his character to do things in this way. He likes to do that, and it's a playful form of teaching that he does. It's just part of his personality. And usually you might, as others have, find it to be rather fun to explore this idea.

Jefferson: Can you have him ask that question again?

Arvantis: When are you going to change the fixture?

Jefferson: Tell him I will do so before a month's time, as I am moving now and many changes are coming, new things are happening, and that will be when I get the new fixture.

Arvantis: He wants you to know that you can do it at any time, and if that is the timing that works best for you then so be it.

Jefferson: Lovely! Tell him I thank him very much for being present with us today. Where are you located right now?

Arvantis: On our planet.

Jefferson: On the same place you were before?

Arvantis: Very much so, yes.

Jefferson: Nice. Do you have any question or any parting thoughts?

Arvantis: We enjoy this interaction immensely and are grateful that you pursue this form of interaction with us, this reconnection that strengthens our bond together, our existence together. It brings forth more awareness that we are one that is part of the all.

The outdated idea that we don't exist is something that for you is diminishing from your beingness. Even within the depths of your psyche you are beginning to let go of that limiting idea more and more such that there are less doubts coming forth from you that at times percolate to the surface and create a bit of an obstacle that slows you down, but that's all right. It's part of the growth process.

We are grateful that you are moving forward and finding our existence to be more real for you, more meaningful, more of a reality that you prefer to exist in, for anyone can choose to exist with this knowledge. We are grateful you are choosing to prefer to be in this reality where our existence is more of a reality for you. The more you choose for it to be real, thus then the more and the easier it is for our vibrations to coexist with yours, to resonate more similarly together so we can in more ways contact one another. Thus then even the day can come when physical contact can occur, face to face, heart to heart communication can occur.

It is with great joy for us that you move forward in this way with greater willingness to define this as a reality, to give it greater credence, more sense of validity, and thus then in doing so you are putting that out and therefore you get back greater opportunities, frequencies, to experience us in more real ways. So, again, with you in this way is a great joy for us. Much love to you!

Jefferson: Wow! Fascinating! It is indeed for me a unique experience to get to know you, and the information we shared today was amazing!

Arvantis: Thank you for being amazed by your amazing self!

Jefferson: All right. Goodbye for now and I will talk to you shortly, very soon!

Arvantis: Very good, until we are together in this way again, much love to you and goodbye!

Jefferson: Thank you very much!

Chapter 4

Excellent Extraterrestrial Experiences, EEE

"We are, and I am, very delighted to have this time to interact with you in this way. It is a great movement forward in bringing about our presence into your world, which is a gift you bring and give to us in that way. So thank you for sharing and interacting in this fashion."

- Arvantis

January 4th, 2010

Arvantis: Very well! It is I, Arvantis, in this moment interacting with you in this sharing. So here we are together in this timing. How is it that you would like to bring forth questions and sharings together dear soul reflection?

Jefferson: Did you know we have a webpage for you, here on Earth?

Arvantis: I am aware! Thank you for putting that together!

Jefferson: How have you been?

Arvantis: Very actively involved with a variety of activities that I find rather endearing to my heart. Playful interchanges with yourself as well as with others upon my own planet!

Jefferson: Oh!

Arvantis: And you? How is it with you?

Jefferson: I am having quite a few awesome synchronicities that are really interesting.

Arvantis: Awesome to hear.

Jefferson: Yeah. Did you give a piggyback ride for a cat on your world?

Arvantis: I have not, no!

Jefferson: What activities have you been involved with?

Arvantis: We had a light show very much like your aurora borealis. It's a wonderful show of lights. Very entertaining. They are lights that have a bit of a sound. Each light has its own note, its own frequency of hum. The light show is quite enjoyable, not only to see but to hear as well. It's like an orchestra from heavens in the sky.

Jefferson: Wow! Hey, can you guys levitate?

Arvantis: I do not. There are some who can who focus on this idea.

Jefferson: What is your work specialty? What is it that you do that you have developed yourself?

Arvantis: I work with physiological activities of living organisms on my planet and on some other planets as well. I study and get to know the functions within the internal systems that make the living organisms able to exist.

Jefferson: Understood!

Arvantis: A little bit like a scientist, a biologist working with living organisms.

Jefferson: So...referring back to what we have spoken about before,

you said you have occasionally visited me, but more often than not I have had some visitors. How often?

Arvantis: What kind of visitors?

Jefferson: Of the extraterrestrial nature!

Arvantis: There are those who visit you in your dream states. You have had a few visitations in that capacity. It can be as frequently as once every month, and there are times where it's more regular in terms of a weekly basis.

Jefferson: Okay. And how many are there that visit me?

Arvantis: There are only a few. There are three to four. They are like guides. They are very close to your functioning in this lifetime. They assist you, and they facilitate some energetic adjustments to your biology, your physiology, as needed, as you allow for and accept and feel are appropriate. Some are very subtle, but occasionally there can be adjustments on a scale in which you would awake in the morning and feel as though something unusual might have occurred, as though things are somehow a little bit different in terms of how you are perceiving your surroundings. But that is all part and parcel with the adjustment, and it is all for your forward movement and is done so in a positive way.

Jefferson: And you mentioned the last time you physically visited me was three-and-a-half months ago. When was the first time? Was it when we went together to Jupiter?

Arvantis: I had interacted with you in other lifetimes. So are you referring to this lifetime specifically?

Jefferson: Yes.

Arvantis: There was a time when you were approximately seven years old. I made contact with you. It was consciousness to consciousness, so it wasn't actually what you would consider seeing me physically. In dream states there were physical appearances, visual contact in that form of your dream states, which then can be like a physical contact, but this was in a dream time, sleep time, consciousness for you.

Jefferson: Okay.

Arvantis: The actual physical contact would have been sometime after your ninth birthday when you were, in a sense, consciously aware of the contact as it was occurring, but when you were through with that contact you then were adjusted with your consciousness so that you don't remember it.

That is something you understand when you are aware and in contact with me or any others. You are agreeable to having memory of that not be accessible when you return back into your normal day to day life there on Earth.

Jefferson: And how tall were you when I first met you?

Arvantis: I was approximately five-and-three-quarters feet in height.

Jefferson: And the first time I saw you, what was my reaction?

Arvantis: That was difficult for you. There was some behavior that is normal for humans who see someone such as an extraterrestrial initially, first time. You did have a bit of faintness occur. You were overwhelmed, in that sense. There was a sense of fright and then you simply, in a wobbly fashion, you slowly fell down from a standing upright position down onto the floor where you began to be in a bit of an altered state of consciousness. A bit of a surreal experience, perhaps, is how you perceived that moment.

Jefferson: Oh.

Arvantis: And after a few moments you began to come to, as it were, as though you had really had a fainting spell. And in time, you began to become more calm and your body, and physiology, and your heart rate began to settle down and you began to remember some things that made it easier for you to feel comfortable with the being I am in front of you. All in all, it took a few hours for you to make the adjustment to a sufficient level in which you could then comprehend what was occurring and be accepting and comfortable with it.

Jefferson: And once I was comfortable with it, what happened?

Arvantis: There were some dialogues, some conversations. You had a little bit of a history shown to you in a form of holographic presentation. Some information was presented to you in that format to give you a little bit of a heads-up on some possible pathways you could perhaps in your future embark upon. It gave you a little bit of background on things that occurred in your life as a very young toddler and even before you were born. You saw interaction amongst your parents, a couple of images of both of them before they met each other. This gave you a little bit more insight on them in ways that they were agreeable to you seeing and experiencing through the holographic visual. That was the primary activity that occurred in that meeting, in that contact, at that timing after your ninth birthday.

Jefferson: And was this in my house, was it somewhere else, was it in a craft?

Arvantis: There was a ship you were upon, yes!

Jefferson: So...when you brought me up to the ship, I was unconscious?

Arvantis: There was an altered state, but you were aware. You were conscious.

Jefferson: Did you speak to me in Portuguese or...?

Arvantis: I spoke to you in a form of language that is similar to telepathy. I do not speak Portuguese, but you would have understood it as though it was Portuguese.

Jefferson: And what language is that?

Arvantis: Again, it is a telepathic language.

Jefferson: Oh.

Arvantis: It is simply an inner language that is a few levels underneath the Portuguese idea or the English idea of language.

Something that you all speak. You are all capable of communicating together on this level of language. But often when you are born you choose to move up into a more specific and focused language level, such as a Portuguese, or French, or German, or Spanish, or English, or Japanese, or Chinese. And in learning that more specific level of language, you often then forget this more expanded level of language, which you all are capable of communicating on together even now in your current day. You have only to remember that it exists and how to access it. And again, it is a form of telepathy.

Jefferson: And I would respond to you in Portuguese or with the same inner language?

Arvantis: You would think of it as speaking like you do in Portuguese.

Jefferson: Hmm.

Arvantis: There is an adjustment made. We do that for you. It brings you back into this more expansive language level. It is something that you really aren't aware of occurring.

Jefferson: Oh, okay. And this was the day that you guys took me to visit other planets or not yet?

Arvantis: That was different—

Jefferson: Oh.

Arvantis: —by a few, hours of your time.

Jefferson: And the other eleven encounters we've had after that first one, they happened with what frequency?

Arvantis: What frequency in respect to what?

Jefferson: How often?

Arvantis: That was in various timings. As we felt and you felt would be most appropriate. They were not set at any regular frequency, no set dates. They were very much based on spontaneous occurrences.

Jefferson: When you are on your world and this spontaneous encounter is going to happen, what are the first signs? How do you know that it's myself calling to you for that event to come to pass? How are the beginnings of the encounters? Are you taking a walk in your world when a thought from me comes to you? How does it work?

Arvantis: It is a little bit like that. Have you ever just had a feeling to call someone? It can be a little bit like that. And there is some overview of where you are and where you have been and there are guides there with you that give us some heads-up on things that are occurring in your life.

Jefferson: Oh.

Arvantis: They can, in a sense, let us know what would be perhaps a timing that would be favorable to interact with you. That is one of the functions that the guides provide. They can let me know and others know when they feel there is something of value that could then be a catalyst to initiate a contact.

Jefferson: Okay. You also said that there are some preparations, some adjustments that are made before you come. What are these adjustments?

Arvantis: Primarily, you will have some adjustments to your schedule so that there will be time for you to have these encounters. There are adjustments made so that you would not miss any planned activities, so you would not be taken out at a moment when it would be necessary for you to be present there.

And there are adjustments in your physiology and psychological states so you will be more receptive to the encounters, so you will be less frightened and more willing to be in that frequency for the interaction and contact to take place. There are times where it is something that really isn't of interest for you to do. So there are adjustments in those areas that can be made if it is in the overall best interest to do so for you in the overall projection of where you want to move forward in your life.

Jefferson: What do you get from these encounters?

Arvantis: I don't really get anything, in that sense. I am simply moving forward in the joy, in the most joyful ways I can. Following, in that sense, the energy that is most uplifting for me to be in and to flourish through and to be a co-creator within.

Jefferson: I see.

Arvantis: So you could say I get more experiences that are enlightened with who I am and that is for me a great joy. I appreciate, and am very grateful, that I am able to tune in to and take actions in ways that are more joyful for me, experiencing greater joy in my life. I do get more of that experiencing through such encounters.

Jefferson: How does it feel to meet a reflection of your soul in a human body, eye to eye?

Arvantis: Quite fascinating! Quite exciting! That's why I do it! That's something I get out of it!

Jefferson: You said you were wearing appropriate attire for the visitation. Can you comment on that attire?

Arvantis: It was like a form of shorts. The fabric is more organic to the material plants on our planet. A bit like cotton on your world. And then I had on a shirt. You could call it a flowing, soft, light fabric that has a very light white coloration with some very colorful threads throughout the fabric. Again, another organic material, the shirt, you could call it. Made of a very organic material similar to that of the shorts.

I had no need for shoes, for again, my feet are very strong. The skin is very thick, soft and flexible, but very thick and strong. It provides a great deal of protection, in that sense, if I were to encounter any sharp objects. The skin is very capable of remaining intact and unscathed or uncut, in that sense.

And I had what you might think of as an amulet that was with a symbol of my planet. It has a vibrant light emanating from it. It is of a blue color, some green, and some shades of color that are unlike what you have on your world. It is approximately the size of a quarter on your world and shaped like a heart, the traditional Valentine hearts you have on your world. It is something that for me is symbolic of my world, for me. It is of my own crafting.

Jefferson: Okay.

Arvantis: It is not a symbol that all in my world would think of as representing our planet.

Jefferson: I see. And...were you wearing glasses?

Arvantis: I do not, no, wear glasses. Did you see someone in a dream that seemed to be an extraterrestrial wearing glasses?

Jefferson: No, not that I remember. I was just wondering. In regards to your eyes, you said they are a mixture of feline and human and that they are bigger than ours. Can you give any other details about them?

Arvantis: They have a large corona, a large top shape to them. They are very flowing within the skull, within the facial features. They fit in smoothly. They don't have a deep indentation, as may be found on your world, that is, they aren't set back as deeply as you tend to find in your world. They do have a bit of a natural coating on them, a bit like a shield for Sun protection. But it is slight, very thin, organic, and it is a membrane that is attached to our biology. We don't remove it, but it can open and close. It has an upper portion and a lower portion. It's a bit like eyelids in how it functions. It provides us with a way to shield out heavy sunlight at particular times on our planet. It also provides a cleaning mechanism. It cleans the surface of the eye. We also have over that a skin layer that is similar to eyelids in your world. And there are tiny hair follicles that are like eyelashes in those of your world.

Jefferson: Okay.

Arvantis: They are very short relative to eyelashes of your world, but ours tend to more densely populated, more of them growing out of the edge of the eyelid's skin.

Jefferson: Okay.

Arvantis: There are various colors to our eyes.

Jefferson: Yes.

Arvantis: And the pupil tends to be a little bit more round than you would find in a cat, but not as quite as round as you have in humans on your world. Not a perfect round pupil.

Jefferson: I see.

Arvantis: And there are some other qualities to the depth of the eyeball. It doesn't go back as deep as those in your world. It isn't perfectly round. It has a little bit of an oblong shape to it, the eyeball. So it isn't quite a round spherical ball. There is a multi-frequency wiring from the eyeball into our, shall we say, central nervous system and that affords us great vision at night.

Jefferson: Oh.

Arvantis: A very acute vision. A very clear night vision relative to how we perceive you in your world see at night. We do not need artificial light to move about very simply and comfortably in our nighttime on our world.

Jefferson: I see. So...the white part of my eye...in your eye is what color?

Arvantis: Well, it's a little bit of a soft shade of a brown. It tends to be a little bit more towards a soft light brown.

Jefferson: Okay.

Arvantis: Some of a yellow, but it is more of a light brown and there is some variation to this that can change over time.

Jefferson: Okay. And the brown part of my eye that is directly around my black pupil, in your eye this area is...is it iridescent green?

Arvantis: There is some of that, yes. There is some blue that is blended in with the green, but the blue isn't in a fixed location within the green. At times the blues can move around a little bit within the green.

Jefferson: I see. And you mentioned there is a bit of yellow as well, where is Jefferson: it?

Arvantis: That tends to be outside of the pupil and green-blue region.

Jefferson: How has our relationship changed since the first time we met?

Arvantis: There is much growth and change, as you create the idea of change to occur. What specifically are you then asking us?

Jefferson: What are these changes?

Arvantis: You live in another country now.

Jefferson: Yeah...but changes in terms of the way we encounter each other.

Arvantis: Changes in terms of your psychology?

Jefferson: Yes.

Arvantis: You are more aware of our existence, more comfortable with us, and you are more willing to accept that.

Jefferson: Yeah.

Arvantis: You are more excited about that. You are in a position to do more of what you prefer which includes sharing ideas about our existence with others on your world. You are more of a support mechanism that can educate people of our presence in your world. This is something that you are more in tune with now and more capable of doing compared to when you were younger.

Jefferson: Oh.

Arvantis: When we first met, you didn't really have the mindset to educate people about us. You wanted others to know we existed, but you didn't have the idea to educate people.

Jefferson: Sure!

Arvantis: Now you have more interest in education of this understanding, of this reality.

Jefferson: Understood! My physical encounters with physical entities of other worlds like yourself has to do with upgrading my physiology as well because of the Earth changes.

Arvantis: Was that a question?

Jefferson: Yes!

Arvantis: It sounded like a statement.

Jefferson: Right! No, yes, but I mean...(Laughter). I will ask you again. Like the upgrades...(Laughter). The upgrades of my physiology have to do with the Earth changes?

Arvantis: That is part and parcel, they work together.

Jefferson: Okay.

Arvantis: You can't have one without the other. They coexist. Together the changes are occurring.

Jefferson: What take has the collective consciousness of humans in allowing or not allowing these encounters to happen?

Arvantis: What changes occurred in consciousness?

Jefferson: No, what take has our collective consciousness, the collective consciousness of humans on Earth, in allowing or not allowing these encounters to happen?

Arvantis: What take?

Jefferson: Yes.

Arvantis: What is take?

Jefferson: *Take,* **meaning: how do they influence whether we can or cannot have encounters with extraterrestrials?**

Arvantis: How does what influence?

Jefferson: The collective consciousness of humans?

Arvantis: Well, the collective can be what determines which direction you will go as a whole.

Jefferson: Oh.

Arvantis: The collective consciousness.

Jefferson: Okay.

Arvantis: If you will, you could consider it to be like one person. Is that person going to go out to the store today, or stay inside, or go for a run, or a swim? What is that person going to do? That person has choice over that. The collective consciousness has that ability too. Are you all, as a collective, going to go out into the cosmos and accept that there are other humans of extraterrestrial origin in this infinite Universe, or are you all going to continue to stay on Earth and consider yourselves to be the only living humanoid form in the Universe?

Jefferson: Okay.

Arvantis: Do you follow that idea?

Jefferson: Yes, very good. Thank you! The other question, since it's one of your specialties, I would like you to quickly touch on the idea of the DNA. We have two strands of DNA correct?

Arvantis: You have several but two are your primary focus at this timing.

Jefferson: Okay. How many strands of DNA is your race primarily focused at this time?

Arvantis: We have five.

Jefferson: What? You have the two that we have and another three?

Arvantis: They are similar, the two, but they are not quite the same. And five is what we function primarily through at this timing.

Jefferson: What would we be able to do if we had five strands of DNA activated?

Arvantis: Well, you could live on our planet. You could be here, and you could associate with those that we interact with very easily. You would be aware of them. It wouldn't be a mystery to you. That would be one thing. Your planet would be quite different. Your world would be quite different. Everything would be quite different. You would be functioning from a more aware state of being, in that sense. Have more access to knowledge, and understanding, and realizational capacity, by having access to five strands activated.

Jefferson: Is it possible that on an individual level, some humans have more strands of DNA activated then others?

Arvantis: Generally, it's only the codons within the strands, the amino acids. There are humans on your world that have more of these, in a sense, awake, alive, turned on, conscious, aware. Not crystallized, not hardened. They are functioning as designed and that then would be the way that the DNA would be more enhanced, in a sense, that it can connect to more of your actual nature. Not better than anyone who doesn't have more amino acids activated, but simply more enhanced, capable of more understanding, and realization, and connection. Can be more deeply with the One, with the Infinite.

Jefferson: Okay.

Arvantis: That then occurs in the amino acids, in the codons. It's a form of, if you will, a form of conscious understanding, awareness, sensibilities, receptivity, transmission capabilities. And so there are those on your planet who are of your Earth origin with the two strands of DNA that have more of these codons activated.

This then is also a collective choice. How many amino acids or codons will be turned on is something that has been collectively agreed upon. There are those who are being born now that will have more of these activated. That is also a collective choice. This increase makes it possible to move forward in this way as a society. The young, the newborns, have more turned on and so they grow up with more expansive ideas, and awareness, and realizations that then evolve into your world's system of definitions and beliefs about who you are and what you are capable of experiencing and creating together.

Jefferson: The adjustments that are done in my biology as a result of our encounters has to do with DNA activation as well?

Arvantis: Yes.

Jefferson: How so?

Arvantis: There are some amino acids and, if you will, codes, kind of like a software program on a computer that are, if you will, uninstalled or simply not being accessed. They are, in a sense, hardened, turned off, crystallized, inaccessible. They aren't part of your primary network. When there are adjustments made, it is as though some of those programs become accessible, part of the network is not crystallized, it's accessible, as though you suddenly are given a password to enter in and utilize that program, that software application, that form of conscious energy within the DNA that allows you to receive and to transmit more expansively, more in alignment with your actual infinite state of being.

Jefferson: Okay.

Arvantis: As though it gave you another source of information and another realm of conscious beings within which to share, and to interact with, and to discover, and to make new friends with, so to speak, to develop new bonds with genetically.

Jefferson: Now, because you are of a feline race, when I contact your

energy, does that make some codons and amino acids in my physical body within my DNA structure awaken, primarily those that are related to the feline race, because I had contact with your physical structure and energy?

Arvantis: There is that initially, yes. That can be part of what is taking place. The more you do that in that direction and the more you tune in to that energy, all the more those codons, those amino acids, become more alive, more aware, more awake, less hardened, less crystallized. If you then step out of that energy, then they will perhaps begin to crystallize back to — if you will as an analogy — ice over like you can have in your northern hemisphere when the glaciers move over land and it gets colder and less inhabited.

Jefferson: So what are, if you can comment on that, the programs that have been installed as a result of our encounters or that were installed and have been activated within me?

Arvantis: It's as though they are already there, you are simply choosing to tune in to them in such a way that it is activating those particular ones, for ultimately there are an infinite number.

Jefferson: Hmm.

Arvantis: Depending on your choices, what you focus on determines which ones will begin to awaken, which ones will begin to generate enough heat and, in a sense, bring warmth into that idea and melt away the glacier, the ice, the crystallization factor so that you can then be in a region that you are willing to comfortably inhabit, that feels comfortable for you and supportive to you.

Jefferson: And those codons of mine that have been awakened as a result of our encounters, what do they allow me to do that I would not be able to do if I had not met you?

Arvantis: To function in this interaction would be primary. Any interaction you are doing with the idea of extraterrestrial existences is part and parcel with that choice.

Jefferson: Oh, I see now.

Arvantis: You could be completely oblivious to the idea of extraterrestrial existence if you chose to move in other directions. Certain codons would be frozen, would "ice over," that relate to matters of our existence. And then you would not be interested in ETs at all. The "landscape" of ETs would not be a region that you would be wanting to inhabit. It would seem cold, and desolate, and lifeless, and you would not venture in that direction to explore the ET reality.

Jefferson: Very well! I have a question here. When someone we admire on Earth is going to be distant for a period of time, we may send them a postcard. Can you pass around a postcard, have everybody write me a short message, and when you come visit me again you could place it on my bed after you leave so when I wake up I can read it?

Arvantis: Oh wonderful. Would you like us to do that?

Jefferson: Yes!

Arvantis: All right then! We will work with you on that idea. That means we will work with you on that idea. It doesn't mean it will be delivered tomorrow.

Jefferson: Okay!

Arvantis: What language would you like it written in?

Jefferson: Ah, probably Portuguese or English. Whatever you feel guided to.

Arvantis: Very well then. We will work with that idea.

Jefferson: Is that possible?

Arvantis: Certainly.

Jefferson: And then, the other idea that I was wondering, in case you wouldn't be able to send a postcard—

Arvantis: One moment.

Jefferson: Yes?

Arvantis: What kind of a picture would you like on your postcard?

Jefferson: Ah, there you are, you see? This was the other idea I had. So perhaps you get someone to draw you and your family?

Arvantis: Certainly.

Jefferson: So you do that as a picture on the postcard.

Arvantis: Lovely!

Jefferson: Then I will know what you and your family look like!

Arvantis: Yes! This sounds quite enticing!

Jefferson: (Laughter). I know right?!

Arvantis: Very well then, we will work with this idea.

Jefferson: In our world we have cameras. Do you have cameras like we do?

Arvantis: They are not quite like yours, but we have devices that serve similar functions.

Jefferson: They capture the moment without having someone to draw, right?

Arvantis: Yes.

Jefferson: So you could have that on the postcard instead of a drawing.

Arvantis: Is that your suggestion?

Jefferson: That is a suggestion, yes!

Arvantis: So you prefer the picture over the drawing?

Jefferson: Yeah, I guess…it shows more details!

Arvantis: What resolution would you like the picture?

Jefferson: The best!

Arvantis: Very well, we will work with you on that idea.

Jefferson: Okay, very good! (Laughter). Where are you today?

Arvantis: I am on my planet. Where I have been for previous channelings, enjoying the outdoors, relaxing by a stream today.

Jefferson: If you are a humanoid, a feline humanoid, I think you may have human DNA and feline DNA. Are there other races that are in your genetic mix that you could comment on?

Arvantis: We have some of the connections that you have within your human DNA.

Jefferson: Okay.

Arvantis: There are then in yours, we understand, at least seven races that compose your DNA, and there could then be considered we have those seven.

Jefferson: Oh.

Arvantis: But then they are supporting some of the primary genetic components in our system that come from other extraterrestrial races that aren't associated specifically with Earth at this timing.

Jefferson: I see. And what makes your skin color light blue?

Arvantis: The genetic material, the information, is primarily what determines that. We, of course, have on some level crafted that energy and information, but being born in this world of ours it generally occurs naturally through the genetic components of information contained therein.

Jefferson: And what is the matter that covers your skeleton structure? Is it flesh like ours? Is it silicon, or a mix, or a completely different material?

Arvantis: It is similar, but it is of a strength that is of a greater bonding than you find generally of humans on your planet. There are forces in our world that require us to have stronger bonds within our skeletal structure and the integument, the tissue, structure as well, for us to maintain our survival here, to be inhabiting the surface of our planet.

Jefferson: What forces?

Arvantis: There are gravitational forces, atmospheric conditions, solar inter-actions, and interplanetary energies, to name a few and to name the primary.

Jefferson: Oh. You said it would take a large amount of time for a person like myself to adapt to the surface of your planet but that it could happen. Does that mean that even my skin would have to go through that change?

Arvantis: Well, yes. That would occur. And there would be some fine tuning necessary of your physiology too. Then, at that point, you could at certain timings on our surface be able to walk freely as you do there.

Jefferson: Okay.

Arvantis: But there are also other conditions and moments on our world where it would not be conducive for you to be out doing such a walk about.

Jefferson: But I could be indoors?

Arvantis: There are shelters that would be capable of supporting you. They wouldn't be like the ones that we generally are in. It would be a modified form of structure that would take into account the variations in your molecular structure.

Jefferson: Oh, I see. But after the adaptation it would be okay?

Arvantis: Again, only at certain timings.

Jefferson: Oh, I see. If I were to do that adaptation there, would I be able to come back and live on Earth?

Arvantis: Then there would be another period of adjustment necessary, but once on Earth, you would be able to walk about at most any time.

Jefferson: So then the physical body would be able to adapt because it has learned how to go back and forth between two different planets?

Arvantis: There would be some of that adaptation built into your system after that, yes. But it would still be necessary, if you were to come back to Revision 5, for some adjustments to take place again.

Jefferson: I see. But when it's the case for visitations, I don't really need to adapt because you can just put a light energy field around my body and that is okay.

Arvantis: That functions nicely, yes!

Jefferson: With that field around the body, a human like myself could not touch an Arkoreun?

Arvantis: There is still contact possible.

Jefferson: Oh alright. Very well. Who is there with you today?

Arvantis: I am here with the form of life that is like a Koala Bear. There are three of them on a tree behind me, on the other side of the stream, approximately fifteen meters away, and they are taking an interest in my presence and I in them as well.

Jefferson: How lovely! If people were to see you there now, would they think you were talking to yourself?

Arvantis: They would understand what I am doing. They know what is occurring. They understand the channeling is taking place. There are those who are not in my surrounding that are, in a sense, viewing, listening in, participating, but not present in the physical space around me.

The animals, the Frupees, would not be listening in. They don't, in our perception, speak a language that we do. But they are aware and we do have a fun and loving relationship. Occasionally they come out and take notice of us and we have a playful interaction. But generally they are more reserved in their interactions.

Jefferson: And what does the sky look like today?

Arvantis: Today it is a bit of brilliant orange with streaks of blue, and the Sun is presently about eleven o'clock in the sky. There are three moons, just now setting. There are, shortly to be, the other moons rising. Those are the primary visuals I see in the sky at the moment.

Jefferson: Okay, do you have any parting thoughts?

Arvantis: Well, again, we are and I am, very delighted to have this time to interact with you in this way. It is a great movement forward in bringing about our presence into your world, which is a gift you bring and give to us in that way. So thank you for sharing and interacting in this fashion!

Jefferson: Okay, and don't forget the postcard!

Arvantis: Yes, we work with you on that.

Jefferson: (Laughter). All right, lovely! Again, thank you very much, and I will talk to you soon.

Arvantis: Much love to you and great joy in your day. Good day!

Jefferson: Good day, thank you!

Chapter 5

Rewriting the "Wrongs"

"As we see and perceive your energies today, you will not destroy, you will not create extinction of your race. You will create a place filled with abundance of joyful experiences in which everyone is in tune with who they are, self governing, and appreciative of their unified world and also appreciative of their unique cultural differences at the same time."

- Arvantis

January 12th, 2010

Arvantis: Very well. Here we are. Soul reflection in communication in physical forms on various physical frequencies. Physical forms of different shapes and size, but still, one soul frequency, one line of communication in which we are able in this moment to share and thus be aware of one another in this way. How are you?

Jefferson: Very excited to be talking to you!

Arvantis: Yes, so joy it is in this way, in this day together! How in this moment then would you like to explore the Infinite that we are?

Jefferson: How do you spell the name of your society?

Arvantis: Well, we don't, but you can in your world spell it as you have, or you can make adjustments so it fits with the way we pronounce it. It's up to you. We do feel that pronouncing it as Arkoreun is generally the way it best translates to your world's language of English. How you spell it is up to you.

Jefferson: Okay. How is the sky in your world right now?

Arvantis: It is lovely! It is a lovely time of evening! The Sun has set and the sky is very glowful. We have a bright purple color in the sky on the horizon where this Sun set, and there is a lengthy visual of the purple at that horizon. As I look up from the horizon towards the sky directly overhead, the color becomes a deeper violet coloration. As I look back even farther, the sky becomes more of a deep blue in quality. And then we do have some variation at the other side, the horizon that is opposite the sunset. There is a bit of a glow from a distant Sun that is casting upon us a bit of an orange hue, and it is very soft and very slight.

Jefferson: Sweet.

Arvantis: So it has been a wonderful day and the evening as well is with quite a bit of flash and flare in a very soothing and comforting way for us. Thank you for asking!

Jefferson: All right! Lovely. What activities have you been engaged in today?

Arvantis: I had a stroll along a stream that is about fifty feet wide and two feet in depth. There are a variety of organic objects in the river including a hearty soil that is almost a form of stone. The stream moves softly and is like a pond with a glassy surface. There are other regions of the stream that move more swiftly.

Today along the stream I had a few of what you might consider friends, although all here on my world are friends, they are the ones who joined me this day as we were taking in the life that is present here in this area. There are trees, some jungle, not a dense jungle. The trees are approximately a hundred meters in height, but they are not densely in their location so there is much sunlight. There is a great deal of vibrant life and sounds of the environment in this region.

So we, in a sense, connect and commune with this life as it communes and connects with us. We share with each other and interact with other things that come to mind, imaginations and sensing of what we are connecting with, of the life forms in this region, as well as ideas that come to us from other worlds. In this way, we enrich each other's experience together in the moment that we shared today. Do you understand that idea?

Jefferson: Yes. Thank you! What is the animal that is closest to you right now?

Arvantis: There are some soft creatures. They are very round. A bit like a turtle you have in the sea or on land. But these do not move like a turtle. They simply are shaped like a turtle in their bodily area. They have what you would consider to be approximately eight to twelve designs along the back of their body that tend to have a rather geometrical quality to them. The number of designs depends on their age. They don't have a hair softness. It's more of a skin that is soft to touch it. They tend to pause if you touch them. They move about the ground with a number of very soft and short legs. The legs are more like a caterpillar in your world.

They do have what you would see as eyes, approximately four in front and a couple towards the back region. The eyes are black but not like a pupil you would find in a human eye. They have a form of antennae around their body that they use like feelers. These are like you would have on a snail, as well as whiskers you would have on a cat. It's a combination of that sort around their exterior.

They are easygoing creatures, very tuned to the plants. They like to live amongst the plants and at times they do get out and crawl around. Especially around the regions of the streams, for there is an abundant source of food and nutrients there that they are attracted to.

Jefferson: How big are they?

Arvantis: They tend to be about the size of a Frisbee on your world, in their larger state. In their smaller state, they are about the size of a plate you would use for a cup of tea, approximately three to four inches in diameter. Their size depends on their age.

Jefferson: Are they scared of Arkoreuns?

Arvantis: There is, in that sense, not a relationship on our world of beings that are frightened of any other being.

Jefferson: Do you have beaches on your world?

Arvantis: We do not have as you have, beaches with large waves. We do have some regions of land that have lakes that aren't large, but there is some beach quality to them, some soft particulate there along the shore where the water and land come together. There is some wave action, but it is very slight. Just a matter of inches, very minimal.

Jefferson: Do you have sand?

Arvantis: There are particulate, there is matter there that is like sand, but it is of a different substance.

Jefferson: Let me ask you someting else. Do you have eyebrows?

Arvantis: I do. They are shaped differently than most humans on your world. They tend to arch up more. They are thin and the hair follicles are very fine, extremely fine. Often times, for some of us, you wouldn't see any coloration because the hair can be so light in color and so fine.

Jefferson: How is it on you?

Arvantis: Yes, it tends to be a bit darker with me and matches the hair that I have which is darker.

Jefferson: And what are they for?

Arvantis: It works as a form of connecting to the environment and alerting us of any particulate, and also it's a way of tuning in to the environment, an additional resource, sensory mechanism, that notifies our biology of what is taking place in our physical environment.

Jefferson: And...is your skin a flesh like ours? I know I asked this question before. I just want to get more details.

Arvantis: It tends to be a different material than you have on your world, and it is in alignment with the environment that we live in. It isn't as soft as you tend to have in your biology. It has more of a durable texture, which is appropriate for the environment that we live in.

Jefferson: Is it made of any material that I could relate to?

Arvantis: There are some qualities that are similar. The endo aspects of them. The fibrous tissue, the cellular structure, the molecular structure and the material of blood. These are similar in a sense. Our biology has veins that carry nutrients through the body. This is something that is similar in that form that you have in your body.

Jefferson: What color is your blood?

Arvantis: It tends to be of a purple quality. When it's exposed to air, it tends to become a very light iridescent purple.

Jefferson: Oh.

Arvantis: It's more of a dark purple in the body when it is not exposed to the air that we have in our environment and the light in our environment.

Jefferson: Okay. Now I would like to talk about something else. What is the last planet you visited?

Arvantis: Well, it would be planet Arkantoreun in the Arcturus region of your astronomical awareness.

Jefferson: You visited a planet in the region of Arcturus and the planet was called...Kantour?

Arvantis: You can refer to it as Arkantoreun or Arkantor, however you prefer.

Jefferson: What brought you there?

Arvantis: There was an opportunity to explore with some of those who are genetically connected to us, that we have at times visited with, and so we were then in that opportunity and enjoyed that visit with them there.

Jefferson: Nice! When was that?

Arvantis: This was approximately five of your days ago.

Jefferson: Wow! Was that the same planet I went?

Arvantis: Not aware of you having been in that location, but maybe you have!

Jefferson: You said there are approximately four extraterrestrials that get in touch with me. Can you tell me their races?

Arvantis: Not at this timing.

Jefferson: I know that one is Zeta!

Arvantis: That is an aspect of you on a parallel reality, very close frequency wise.

Jefferson: And he has visited me physically?

Arvantis: This has occurred.

Jefferson: How many times?

Arvantis: Approximately, at this point, twelve.

Jefferson: It's a coincidence that it's the same amount of time that you have visited me!

Arvantis: If you say it's a coincidence!

Jefferson: What else could it be?

Arvantis: It could be simply that it has occurred twelve times in both instances.

Jefferson: Okay. And where is he from?

Arvantis: He is from a region in Sirius. A world that is far from its prior state of existence in the sense that it once was a thriving society, not to different from the one on the world you live in today. But it is something that, if you were in your same timeline now and to visit, it would be quite extinct. You will find there are many changes that have occurred to that world, even over the time span of your current lifetime on this planet.

Jefferson: What changes?

Arvantis: It has gone through a number of geological storms, in a sense.

Jefferson: Ah...

Arvantis: A rebuilding and regenerating of ground matter and the atmosphere, for there was much toxic radiation of a sort in that environment that is now, in a sense, self cleansing to a new state, renewed state, so that it will once again be able to sustain life as you are most familiar with on your world.

Jefferson: Are they suffering?

Arvantis: They do not live on that planet in this time and day anymore. They are out in the world, basically in crafts and there are a few other planets, in a sense, that they have moved to and inhabited that aren't of their original, in a sense, native birthplace.

Jefferson: And, how old is he?

Arvantis: He is of an age that frequency wise is in alignment with your current age.

Jefferson: So they moved from their planet to another planet and they are living on their crafts?

Arvantis: They have scattered about into two different regions. Not just one location.

Jefferson: And why is it that he comes and visits me?

Arvantis: To be able to, in a sense, right the wrongs, in a sense, not that there is any right or wrong from the Universal perspective, but the idea that in their society they made choices that were rather cataclysmic and brought destruction, as you would generally define the idea of destruction.

In his interaction with you there is, in a sense, there is opportunity to go back in time to a different timeline and make different choices so there will be different results in their future. Interacting with you affords him the opportunity to make different choices so then in the future their world will not be desolate, will not be a planet that is undergoing regeneration from the cataclysmic actions they had once taken in the prior timeline in the alternate reality from which they come.

Jefferson: Oh my Gosh. When was the last time he visited me physically...oh you said...yeah, three months ago!

Arvantis: That was last time that I visited you. Approximately, three-and-a-half months ago.

Jefferson: Yeah, what about him?

Arvantis: There was opportunity for him to have been there within the month. This may have occurred, but we don't keep track of all of his movements. And we are not receiving any information to suggest otherwise at this timing.

Jefferson: So he has been here within a month's time?

Arvantis: It would appear that he has within the last month visited with you, but we do not follow all of his movements.

Jefferson: And is his race more evolved than ours?

Arvantis: On certain areas, but in other areas they have their lessons, you could say, to learn.

Jefferson: Oh.

Arvantis: And they are doing quite well with learning!

Jefferson: And how does he get here? With a spacecraft?

Arvantis: That is a form of travel for them, yes.

Jefferson: Okay. Is he as tall as I am?

Arvantis: He tends to be shorter in stature, and weight, and size.

Jefferson: Okay. And the other people that have visited me, physically, we can't talk about right now?

Arvantis: There will be time when you will have opportunity to learn more of them.

Jefferson: Okay. How about the idea of the postcard? How is it going?

Arvantis: That is something we are still working with.

Jefferson: Oh. Did you tell your family about it?

Arvantis: There is understanding with those who would be manifesting that and assisting manifesting that with you. There is all who need to know, in that sense, aware of the idea. But you know, sometimes you put a letter in the mail and it doesn't always get there the next day.

Jefferson: (Laughter). Well, the idea was for you to bring it with you the next time you were here.

Arvantis: It is something we are working on.

Jefferson: When I asked before, "is it possible to leave a postcard," you said you are going to work with me. What does that mean?

Arvantis: That means it is in development stages. The manifestation of that has not yet occurred, but the manifesting is underway.

Jefferson: And is the process something you can share with us?

Arvantis: It is a matter of what you have in your world of delivering a postcard to someone and then having others along the way carry it to them, to the destination. It is somewhat similar to that. But there is other protocol because this is a particular type of contact with extraterrestrials and in your world that has very specific requirements that need to be followed. Those are ideas that can be very complex and are then things that we simply have no necessity at this timing to inundate you with.

Jefferson: Can you give me some timeframe?

Arvantis: That is not present, no.

Jefferson: Okay. Who is there with you as far as Arkoreuns?

Arvantis: There are several present who are listening in and partaking in this interaction this day of our time together.

Jefferson: Do you have any other visitors on your planet at this time?

Arvantis: There may be some on another region but not any present with us in this location.

Jefferson: When someone visits your planet at a different location than where you are, are you able to sense that there is a visitation occurring and who they are?

Arvantis: There can be. There can be an awareness by someone on our planet that it is taking place but not necessarily by all of us on our planet.

Jefferson: And you don't have monetary exchange as we do, right?

Arvantis: That is correct.

Jefferson: Did you start like that or did you have to go through change?

Arvantis: We had societies before us that could be considered our predecessors from which we have evolved that had some similar forms of exchange established, but not to the extent that you would find in your world. They didn't have the detail, and the complexity, and the lack of open, clear, visible awareness of what was taking place in all of those, if you will, financial exchanges. They had a very integral based system that was transparent for all who partook to see.

There were no complexities to cloud or shelter transactions. There was nothing that would prevent others from knowing what was taking place in our financial exchange systems.

Jefferson: Do you have a society where all are provided for and all may be blessed and enriched by the lives of everybody else?

Arvantis: We have all that we need, yes, and everything everyone does really does bless the lives of everyone else no matter what it may be they are doing.

Jefferson: And tell me about your technology. Do you create something new everyday that can support you to live a life that is more comfortable, more interactive?

Arvantis: We have very little of what you would consider technology. We do have some functions that are for travel in some capacity. It could be considered technology. We do have some image capture devices that could be considered technology. We do have some recording and archival devices that could be considered technology. There isn't much else on our world you might think of as technological devices.

We are capable of interacting and sustaining ourselves without any technology. We do experiment with various devices, but we are fully aware that they are not things we need in order to function, and experience life, and enjoy who we are.

Jefferson: I see. Can you comment on where Earth is 357 years in the future?

Arvantis: From your present timeframe?

Jefferson: Yes.

Arvantis: We perceive that it will have made a number of adjustments in terms of the social structure, the governmental structure, your financial structure, your medical structure, and your educational structure. Your cultures will be integrated in a way in which everyone is nurturing everyone. There will still be differences between regions, especially geographical regions, in terms of preferences artistically, musically and in terms of dietary interests. There will still be cultural uniqueness.

Overall, there will be a unified humanity, and there will be forms of abundance to include all. There will be abundant forms that will be enjoyable by all. You will no longer have your ideas of lack. Your ideas of poverty will no longer exist. Your ideas of crime will no longer exist. Your institution of prisons will no longer exist!

Jefferson: Yeah!

Arvantis: Your system of litigation and law, as you see it now with the legal cases and law suits in court rooms, will no longer exist either. You will have more forms of technology than what we have in our world. There will be the ability for your society to interact and to travel off your planet, even outside of your solar system. You will be guides and teachers to people on other planets, just a few at that timing.

You will have a greater sense of understanding that you are the creators. You are the source of All That Is in your experience in every moment. You will not be living in a world that believes there is something outside of you that is responsible for your fate or your destiny. You will realize that you are the ones responsible for all that you are experiencing and that everything is connected to all things and is of great joy. All things can be experienced joyfully.

The ideas of conflict will cease to exist at that timeline on your planet, as we perceive your energies today. For you can change and go different directions and even go about paths that bring about a state in which there is no life left on your planet 357 years from now. But as we see and perceive your energies today, you will not destroy, you will not create extinction of your race. You will, as we said earlier, create a place filled with abundance of joyful experiences in which everyone is in tune with who they are, self governing, and appreciative of their unified world and also appreciative of their unique cultural differences at the same time.

Jefferson: Wow! You spoke before about the idea that a month ago there was "a window" for the Zeta being to come and visit me. Can you comment on this window? Who creates it? How does it come to happen?

Arvantis: It is one of the mysteries of life and something that the Zetas are more in tune to recognizing. How such windows of opportunity come to exist is part of the mystery of the more expansive mind, the heart being that you are as the one that is the all. How any of us go about creating such a window from the higher and more expansive levels is something that is still a bit of a mystery even from our realm of awareness. We acknowledge that it is us, that it is you, that is creating that, but just how you go about it isn't always something you are going to be aware of in your present incarnation, in your present level of awareness. That you create it on a deeper and more expanded level of your beingness is something we know without a doubt does occur.

There are things we experience that we know we create, but we don't always delve in to and try to determine exactly, "how did we do this?" We simply appreciate that we are experiencing a mystery of our own higher creator-self's magical wizardry. We let it unfold into our moment to moment experiencing where we can relish, appreciate, and rejoice in the creation of it. What we put out is what we get back, but rather than analyzing it all, we simply let it be a joyful moment.

Jefferson: You also said that there are some adjustments that are done, and when I asked about them you said that one of them is that you communicate with my guides and see how it's going and what has happened so far. Does this mean you check in with them?

Arvantis: This is something that occurs, generally, yes, certainly!

Jefferson: How do you communicate with my guides?

Arvantis: There is a form of telepathy.

Jefferson: Have you met them already?

Arvantis: We have some communication, yes. There are some guides you have that are non-physical in which we will not meet in terms of physical contact.

Jefferson: Okay. What guides have you met physically?

Arvantis: Physically, at this time, we will only indicate we have met the one that is, that you think of as Zeta, that is very close, that has the opportunity at times to interact with you. We are in physical contact with that being, frequently, but not in all moments. There have been some other contacts with some other of those physical guides in your realm, but again, we will leave that for another time.

Jefferson: Okay. So you have already met the aspect of me that is a Zeta?

Arvantis: I have.

Jefferson: No, I mean physically.

Arvantis: We have had physical contact.

Jefferson: How? Did he go to your planet or you went to his?

Arvantis: We had a contact on your world. There was also another time that we met that relates to this idea as well that was in a craft that was in space, if you will. Not on a planet.

Jefferson: So you came to our Earth and you both talked?

Arvantis: We had the communication telepathically, primarily.

Jefferson: And did you go to his craft or he went to yours?

Arvantis: There was a craft that was, in a sense, like what you would find in the Yahyel that is similar to that which was over the Phoenix Lights where there are a number of extraterrestrial societies that can board and interact. It is a bit like a spacecraft of consciousness. It can appear to be physical, a metal structure, but it is primarily a construct of living form, the craft itself. And then there are many extraterrestrial races onboard that are interacting with one another at any given moment for various reasons. It is a bit of a vacationland, if you will, for various races to visit, and to relax, and to encounter, and to learn about their infinite existence as it exists in other life-formats, other races of humans and non-human physiological life forms.

Jefferson: So the Association of Worlds has a resort established in space and other beings that are a part of it can come in and interact with each other.

Arvantis: There are these, yes, more than one.

Jefferson: And that day that you interacted with this aspect of me that is Zeta, did you go there specifically to meet him or did you meet him when you were there by coincidence or synchronicity?

Arvantis: It was a planned meeting.

Jefferson: Oh, I see. And both of you saw that a meeting like that was an expression of the highest excitement of both of you?

Arvantis: That is something you could consider yes.

Jefferson: And can you comment on what that meeting was for?

Arvantis: We were choosing to bring about a cohesive interaction with you, the best we could that would bring about the most uplifting results for all involved. And we felt it would be good to have contact vibrationally, frequency wise, in our physicality. This would then give you a greater sense of physical vibrational recognition and comfort when we have interactions with you, both physically and non-physically. Contact in forms such as this dialogue are a non-physical interaction with you.

The vibrational continuity that is established through his and my physical contact carries through in our interactions with you. It makes a stronger frequency bond, and when we interact with you it's easier for you to tune in to, easier for you to feel more comforted with it, which allows you to relax even more and tune in to it even more. You then are able to hear things more clearly and to come about with ideas and to move in directions that will be more in alignment with what you will find most joyful, most revealing, most exciting.

Jefferson: How long was it?

Arvantis: It was very brief, approximately four of your hours.

Jefferson: Brief? Wow. And uh...did you shake hands?

Arvantis: This was not necessary. There was, in that sense, no bodily contact necessary.

Jefferson: What does he look like?

Arvantis: He looks just a little bit like what you would think of as a human on Earth. He is smaller, lighter, thinner, not having the hair, not having the same color of skin. The eyes are larger and they have a dark coating, shielding, like sunglass over the eyes. The nose is smaller. The ears are smaller. The body and bone structure are slighter.

Jefferson: How many fingers?

Arvantis: There is one less finger than you have.

Jefferson: Oh, okay. And does he have an eyebrow?

Arvantis: Not what I would consider an eyebrow. There is a bit of a soft ridge, a soft protrusion of skin in that region.

Jefferson: Oh, I see. And do you know the color of his eyes?

Arvantis: That was something that I did not have contact with.

Jefferson: Sure, sure, sure.

Arvantis: But I would imagine it would be a tint of a dark blue. That would be my sensing.

Jefferson: Do you know what he does, like you are a scientist?

Arvantis: He spends all of his time out on the dock fishing for mackerel.

Jefferson: No...seriously.

Arvantis: You don't think that is a serious answer?

Jefferson: Sure...no.

Arvantis: Why not?

Jefferson: Uh...that he spends his time fishing?

Arvantis: Why would he not conduct himself in such a manner?

Jefferson: I don't know, there are so many things to explore...

Arvantis: Perhaps he is hungry and has a sweet tooth for mackerel.

Jefferson: (Laughter). No...seriously...do you know what he does?

Arvantis: He is frequently focused on adjusting the frequency of the world in which he came, in that sense, to align it back into choices that can be more favorable for his future world, alternative futures outcome in that way. He is interacting with those, especially you and others on your planet, to make the adjustment more of a reality.

Jefferson: You said before that...well...before I ask you that...if he is an aspect of myself and you are my future self, is he connected to you as well?

Arvantis: There is that connection, yes.

Jefferson: So he is a sort of past self?

Arvantis: There is ability to define it that way.

Jefferson: How far in my future is he from?

Arvantis: The timeline isn't that necessary to understand in the nature of this interaction, in the nature of this his being another aspect of myself, in that sense.

Jefferson: Oh.

Arvantis: The idea of him being a past or future self isn't something that really applies in this particular other-self matter. It's a little bit more of a timeless-self, same-self aspect.

Jefferson: Wow!

Arvantis: It's a different idea of time than what you have been taught to understand in your world.

Jefferson: Okay. How tall is he?

Arvantis: He is going to be in the neighborhood of four to five feet depending on which timeline he is interacting with you from.

Jefferson: Wow, that's fascinating. I know what you mean; at different ages he is going to be different heights.

Arvantis: That would apply to the difference in size, primarily, yes.

Jefferson: And do you plan things that you are going to do in the future.

Arvantis: I usually haven't that need to plan ahead, for the moment is where I focus and experience most of my life.

Jefferson: Do you know when it's going to be the next time we are going to connect with each other like this?

Arvantis: I at times have a sensing, but it isn't something I always have to plan for, or ever have to plan for. It simply will unfold in the timing that is most appropriate.

Jefferson: How long do you think it will take before we meet in a way that I can introduce you to other people as my Arkoreun friend?

Arvantis: I would give it between ten to twenty-five years.

Jefferson: Ten years, that's it?

Arvantis: Ten to twenty-five.

Jefferson: Fantastic!

Arvantis: The idea would suit you better if you give yourself more flexibility around the idea as it relates to our meeting one another.

Jefferson: How so?

Arvantis: There are continual fluxes and changes that relate to that timing of meeting.

Jefferson: Sure, sure!

Arvantis: That can then alter the actual, physical, contact day of meeting.

Jefferson: How can I be more flexible about that?

Arvantis: To allow it to occur when it is appropriate. To be open to it fluctuating in terms of the actual day of occurrence. Do not try to get the day cast in stone or written down on a calendar so you could look forward to and expect on that date it will occur.

Jefferson: Okay, well, we have just a couple of minutes to go. Do you have anybody else around you that would want to ask a question?

Arvantis: Oh, one moment.

{...a brief moment of silence...}

Arvantis: There is an expression of deep love, vibrational support, for the adjustment in your physical world that you are undertaking by moving from your San Francisco region to the Brazil region. There is much adjustment in terms of the geological energies that you will be exposed to, and you are perfectly capable of making that adjustment. There are the psychological frequencies as well that will be something you will be able to make the adjustment with. There is, with us, a large vibrational illuminating energy of love and support in consciousness to assist in that change, in that taking up roots from San Francisco and moving to Brazil. Much support vibrationally here for you in that process, in that change to a new location. We wish you well. We know the new location will support you in the ways that will be of greatest joy for you.

Jefferson: So the energy that exists in Brazil is completely different?

Arvantis: Not completely, but there are variations. They are sufficient enough for adjustments needing to occur, and will occur, some without your awareness. Others you will be aware of. It is something you will be able to move through, generally without any extra effort on your part.

Jefferson: And as far as visitations from you guys, does it matter what place I am?

Arvantis: There will perhaps be a little more of an opening there. But that's no reason then to feel fixated on staying in any particular one region.

Jefferson: Why is it that there are more openings there?

Arvantis: There are geological differences that are more conducive to that type of interaction, in some regions not far from where you are planning to initially move to.

Jefferson: Okay. Very well. So my last question, can you hint on what are the fixtures that your brother was talking about?

Arvantis: Some of your phrases and expressions, it's a bit like a mini-attitude that you have. Mini phrases, mini, short, m-i-n-i, mini. Not m-a-n-y. Short phrases that you have that are like fixtures in the house, they remain. You don't notice them, but they are present like a light fixture overhead. It's there, but you don't always notice it. You have mini phrases, short phrases, that are like fixtures. You don't see them. You speak them, but you are not aware of them. There are those then that he was talking about.

So you can take the idea that he spoke of in that prior channeling and then apply this new information to what he was saying. It has to do with short phrases that you speak out without realizing, like the light fixture over your head that you don't realize it is there. In a sense, you take it for granted. You don't recognize what it is that is coming out, what its function might be, how it might shed a light on others who are present under that light, others who are hearing that short phrase who are then being cast into that light, if you will, of the phrase you speak. As though the phrase itself was like a light fixture, a light bulb, and when you speak, it is as though the light is turning on and casting a glow on those present in the room, or those who are present by hearing the short phrase you speak. Become aware of this light fixture, these short phrases.

There are some, as you become aware of, they will shed a light upon your dialoguing with others in a way that we and he feels will be more beneficial for you. In time you will become aware and recognize this.

There is, in this way that he likes to do, a lesson for you if you will, if you choose to, open that book and explore. Not that you have to. Not that it is a "lesson that you have to learn in life." But it is like a small lesson book that you can open up and explore and excitedly read about, learn, recognize and grow from.

Jefferson: Is it possible for me to hear your voice in my head?

Arvantis: That is something you can meditatively work on developing, yes.

Jefferson: When you say "meditatively," do you mean sitting down and quieting my mind and having that intention?

Arvantis: Yes. And you can imagine conducting a conversation with me as you are doing now. Let it just be an imagination, a playful exercise. You don't have to write anything down or record anything that you think may have been said. Just let it be an exercise or, if you will, a form of play.

Jefferson: Okay.

Arvantis: And if you want to work with it more than once, it can form a more concise ability in the future to channel me directly if that becomes something you want to do.

Jefferson: Can I hear your voice...like you would be standing in my room talking to me, is that possible?

Arvantis: Imagine.

Jefferson: Okay.

Arvantis: Imagine! Imagine. You will not hear through your physical ears. You will hear it in your mind, in that sense. Imagine in your mind you can hear tonal quality, variation from one voice, one person, to the next. You will begin to hear my voice. It might sound a little bit differently for it may be coming from a different place. It doesn't have to have the same vocal quality as you hear now for it will be coming from a different place. So it might sound different for you.

Jefferson: Hmm.

Arvantis: Do you follow that idea?

Jefferson: Coming from a different place...an inter-dimensional place?

Arvantis: Yes.

Jefferson: Okay.

Arvantis: It will sound different than how you actually hear me now. But the idea is, if you want to hear me then this would be one form to develop that connection.

Jefferson: Great, fantastic! It is time to go. Do you have any parting thoughts?

Arvantis: That you ask the question is an indication that your higher mind is giving you a clue, an indication, a signal, a tool to work with, to build up this bond that in the future would make it possible for you to channel me directly. How will you move forward with this clue that your higher mind has brought into your aware state? You don't have to move forward with it. You don't have to begin trying in meditative states to have these conversations with me, but it is something your higher mind is bringing to you as a tool you have available now to work with. It is up to you whether you choose to move forward in that way. If you do, it will be beneficial in strengthening your ability in the future to channel me directly. Always in these ways, we suggest that you follow your greatest joy. Let that be your ultimate guide.

Jefferson: You mean channel you...like Shaun is channeling you?

Arvantis: Yes.

Jefferson: Wow, that is awesome! All right. Well, fantastic! So Arvantis, thank you very much. I look forward to meeting you again, to going and visiting other planets with you again, and for our postcard!

Arvantis: Yes, thank you! Much joy sharing and interacting with you in this way. Those here with me want you to know there will be much joy and love and energy sent to support you in the move. We ask that you allow it to be of great joy for you. Know that it is a great step forward for you. Know that you can always move back into North America at some point in the future if that is what your heart desires. It is always a choice that will be available again.

Let yourself flow joyfully with the choices you make enrichingly and supportively! Stand strong in your choice any moment that it comes from your heart's desire. We thank you, and we look forward to that next time we have in this format to interact with you dear one. There is with you much joy, much love, and we bid you a fond farewell from San Francisco. Until we see you again in your native Brazil. Goodbye, good day, and good sleeping!

Jefferson: Thank you very much!

Chapter 6

Soul Mates, Twin Flames & One Night Stands

"We are enjoying our world, our life, our interactions, and we are expanding our ability to communicate with realms and societies such as yours. It brings us great joy!"

- Arvantis

February 2nd, 2010

Arvantis: Wonderful to be in this moment with you together to communicate and share in ways that bring us new joys and new understanding, new ways to experience our infinite soul reflection together. How are you?

Jefferson: It is lovely to have the opportunity to speak to my soul reflection again!

Arvantis: Wonderful to be with you now in this moment, in this fashion of communication! Delightful to interact with you! How would you like to move forward together in this timing?

Jefferson: Other than the Zeta being, do you communicate with any other soul reflection of myself at this timing?

Arvantis: We have at times done so, yes, other lifetimes, yes! There are other lifetimes in which you exist. We have communicated to you on those.

Jefferson: So you have communicated with another aspect of me that is not the Zeta being and is not myself?

Arvantis: Yes.

Jefferson: Who with?

Arvantis: You on other timelines.

Jefferson: As a human or...?

Arvantis: Yes!

Jefferson: Oh, but that would be Giordano Bruno.

Arvantis: We have had contact with that you on that timeline, yes.

Jefferson: And right now, in this lifetime of yours, are you communicating with me in another timeframe?

Arvantis: There is that, you could define it that way, yes?

Jefferson: What timeframe?

Arvantis: That would be on another lineage, a frequency approximately 1814 of your calendar dating system.

Jefferson: 1814 in the future or in the past?

Arvantis: That would be the year on the calendar of your calendar system, 1814.

Jefferson: Oh, and who am I?

Arvantis: That is something that you will not be aware of in this lifetime yet, and it isn't necessary for you to know. We thank you for the question.

Jefferson: All right. You spoke about the Yahyel a little bit before. Can you expand on your society's relationship with them?

Arvantis: We have some contact with them in the area of facilitating the awakening of people here on Earth to who they are as Earth humans.

Jefferson: Okay. When did it start and how, your relationship with them?

Arvantis: Yes, that is something that will be more detailed when we have more time to talk in person with you. More information will come through when we have the ability to sit down and explore life together in the physical realm.

Jefferson: Oh...I see. When will that be?

Arvantis: That will be within one to two-and-a-half decades, as we see your energies now.

Jefferson: Oh I see...yeah, thank you. Tell me, how did you meet Ishuwa?

Arvantis: That is something that will come through at that timing as well.

Jefferson: Oh, okay. When was the last time you went to his planet?

Arvantis: That is something that will come through as well at that timing.

Jefferson: In ten years from now?

Arvantis: One to two-and-a-half decades of your timing.

Jefferson: Okay. What is it that can come through now about his society?

Arvantis: What was that question?

Jefferson: What is it that can come through now about his society?

Arvantis: Whose society?

Jefferson: The Yahyel society!

Arvantis: You can have a channeling session with them and ask all you would like to know about them. It's more appropriate to do it in that route.

Jefferson: In terms of your relationship with them, what can you tell us today?

Arvantis: Yes, we have a wonderful supportive relationship to facilitate the awakening of Earth humans to understand more of who they are.

Jefferson: Wonderful! I know you can breathe in our atmosphere, but what would happen if the spacecraft were to leave you behind?

Arvantis: Yes, that could happen but it won't!

Jefferson: That could happen, really?

Arvantis: We would perhaps be made a movie of.

Jefferson: What?

Arvantis: Whoever got left behind, perhaps you would make a movie about that individual that was left behind.

Jefferson: I see. Would you be able to survive on Earth?

Arvantis: That is something that wouldn't be appropriate for our physiology for an extended period of time, no.

Jefferson: Oh, I see. So even if you were to undergo an adaptation you still wouldn't be able to live here?

Arvantis: If we were to go where?

Jefferson: If you were to undergo an adaptation period...

Arvantis: It wouldn't be something that we would do. If we were left on the planet without any connections to our society, then there would no longer be a sustaining level for our physiology to maintain itself for an extended period of time on your planet's surface. Unless there have been provisions set out in advance for a long extended stay to take place.

Jefferson: Oh...I see. And other than the food you eat, what other types of nourishment keeps your body healthy?

Arvantis: Well, our bodies are always healthy, in that sense. It does exactly what it's designed to do. So we simply follow our heart and our joy, and do in each moment as best we can that which feels most enticing and uplifting. That allows our body to always be in its optimal state of functioning.

Jefferson: Oh. Do you guys have what we call breakfast, lunch, and dinner?

Arvantis: We have food. We have sit down times together, occasionally, but not as regularly as you do on your world. We don't eat three meals a day as you referred to in the idea of breakfast, lunch, and dinner.

Jefferson: Okay.

Arvantis: We generally will have nourishment in the early hours. Sometimes during the day there will be some intake of some form. That usually is sufficient.

Jefferson: I see. So you eat in the morning, you take your breakfast first thing, and then you don't eat anymore?

Arvantis: We have some nourishment in the morning and then sometimes at some point during the day we might have something as well. But not always. It varies from day to day and person to person.

Jefferson: Do you eat the same thing every day?

Arvantis: Not the same thing. There is always something quite new, and delicious, and enjoyable, and satisfying!

Jefferson: What time is it in your world right now?

Arvantis: We have recently had a sunrise. Approximately one-quarter up from the horizon to directly overhead is where our Sun is currently located. One-quarter of the rise. That is all it has made in its elevation through the sky on its path overhead today.

Jefferson: Are you aware of a person that we on Earth know as Bashar, and his people?

Arvantis: I am familiar with this individual, yes, and the Sassani society.

Jefferson: Have you met him personally?

Arvantis: I have had some interaction, yes.

Jefferson: Like...in the physical?

Arvantis: There has been some physical interaction, yes.

Jefferson: Where?

Arvantis: That would be something that occurred on a spaceship where there were several societies together, interacting with one another.

Jefferson: And have you spoken to him?

Arvantis: Yes.

Jefferson: Can we know what you guys were talking about?

Arvantis: There were a variety of topics. There isn't, in that sense, something we have at mind to share at this moment.

Jefferson: And what does he look like?

Arvantis: What does he look like?

Jefferson: Yeah.

Arvantis: He looks like a human extraterrestrial. Not someone you generally see on your world. He is someone who is of a smaller size than myself, certainly. And has a smaller physical frame or body. Body is not quite the size of those in our society by a number of feet. The appearance is something we are quite familiar with, for there are quite a number of other races of extraterrestrials that have similar sizes, and shapes, and appearances as him, as those in his world of the Sassani.

Jefferson: Does he wear clothes?

Arvantis: That is something that in the interactions in which I had experienced, there were no clothes, in that sense. Not anything that was considered necessary. Not anything unusual about that.

Jefferson: And what color is he?

Arvantis: He had a slight grayish color, a white-gray skin coloration, at the timing of my interaction with him.

Jefferson: When was that?

Arvantis: That would have been approximately fourteen of your years ago.

Jefferson: Wow…and have you spoke to him about Earth at all?

Arvantis: This is something we have a familiar conversational topic about, yes. Something we discuss, yes.

Jefferson: Have you been to Earth since last time you told me you were here?

Arvantis: I may have been, but it isn't something that we are going to see on the radar screen, if you will.

Jefferson: Can you elaborate on that?

Arvantis: There is no radar screen identification of our visitation. Nothing in your world, no technology that would have been able to observe our presence with its radar technology. It would not have known that we were present when we made our visitation.

Jefferson: Hmm. So when you say you made a visitation, was it an official visitation or you just came to visit me?

Arvantis: There are various reasons for such visitations. We have had a large group come through and stop over to interact with several in your world. You were one of those, and I was one to interact with you. That has occurred, yes.

Jefferson: When?

Arvantis: That was approximately three-and-a-half of your months ago...a little bit longer now...closer to four months ago?

Jefferson: Oh, but that...that was the receivership!

Arvantis: Yes!

Jefferson: I see, so after that you didn't visit me?

Arvantis: There may have been.

Jefferson: Oh. I...can you give me some leeway here, given my human understanding, when you say that you "may have," what does that mean?

Arvantis: That means there is no definitive answer coming forth at this timing, so you will have to work with the idea and the curiosity in another way.

Jefferson: Okay, well...let me talk about this then. In your world, when you are interested in dating a woman, what do you do?

Arvantis: We have interactions with them in the ways that we feel most enlightened and of joy to do. What do you do?

Jefferson: Oh, we do like…so many things! How do you tell her that you are interested in her?

Arvantis: We have communication and let her know.

Jefferson: Okay.

Arvantis: Is that too complicated?

Jefferson: You simply speak to her?

Arvantis: Is that too complicated, do you understand that idea?

Jefferson: That you have communications?

Arvantis: Yes! We simply tell her.

Jefferson: Yeah, but like what, do you give her a flower?

Arvantis: You just tell her.

Jefferson: Oh. Don't you do anything else, like you call her for a ride on a spacecraft?

Arvantis: No, we simply explain to that person how we feel about them in the interaction in the moment that we become aware of the sensation. No need for flowers or special activities. We don't need to dance about and flap our wings, so to speak, and show off vibrant colors. That is one way, but it is not the way we function.

Jefferson: Do you believe, or subscribe, or relate to the concept of soul mates and twin flames?

Arvantis: This is something your world is very focused on. It isn't something that we have interaction with in our world. We simply interact in each moment and follow our hearts.

Jefferson: You don't?

Arvantis: We understand this is something you have on your world, but in our world it isn't something we have.

Jefferson: What do you mean, it's not something you have?

Arvantis: We simply interact with the people who are in front of us in any given moment and follow our heart. Whoever is there is the soul mate, whoever is there is a twin flame. We don't have to label them as being any different or somehow more special than any other person we have interaction with. They are all special; they are all soul mates. We are following our heart. That they are there lets us know that is the most appropriate soul mate and twin flame to be interacting with in that moment. They are the special one in that moment or they wouldn't be in our life in that moment.

Jefferson: So you don't necessarily agree with or go with the idea that when a soul is created it is separated into two polarities and then it will grow back together?

Arvantis: You can create a world with that. It's not a matter of agreeing or disagreeing. It's simply what reality you want to live within. You can create a reality where that idea exists, but it isn't necessary. It's not the only reality.

Jefferson: I see! Do you have what we would consider a one-night stand? Like you call a girl or the girl calls you and then you go out and you spend the night with her and that's it?

Arvantis: We have interactions that can be very brief. We don't label it as a one- night stand.

Jefferson: But what I mean is...sexual interaction!

Arvantis: We have interactions that can be of a very intimate nature.

Jefferson: And are they brief, like you find a woman, then you have this intimacy and then you don't see each other anymore?

Arvantis: Well, we don't necessarily find. It's not like we go looking for. We simply follow our heart. In a moment where there is someone else who comes into our experience and we have those sensations together, it might be for a short period of time. We might not see that person again throughout our entire lifetime, but we are simply following our heart in that exchange, in that type of relationship.

Jefferson: Oh. So you said you have a girlfriend, right?

Arvantis: There are those that I interact with who are of the female aspect, and they are friends.

Jefferson: But do you have someone that is like a companion, like a wife.

Arvantis: I have someone that I interact with on a regular basis, but we don't have marriage.

Jefferson: So if you feel like making love with another girl, would your girlfriend, so to speak, be mad at you?

Arvantis: Why would something occur in that way in our world?

Jefferson: Sorry?

Arvantis: Why is there any reason to get angry?

Jefferson: Well, if I am going out with one person that wants me to only go out with her, then she might get angry if I dated someone else.

Arvantis: And how do you feel about that?

Jefferson: I feel that it's off.

Arvantis: Does it allow you to follow your heart if you do that?

Jefferson: No!

Arvantis: As we said, we only follow our heart. So there is no experience of trying to own another person and tell them they can or cannot do a particular thing. That would not be allowing for that other person to follow their heart. That would be trying to restrict, to place limitations on an aspect of oneself, which is symbolically presenting itself as that other person in that relationship.

We don't live in a society where we place expectations and limitations on ourselves, nor on others who "seem" to be other people but are actually just ourself from another point of view of Existence. We allow for ourself to follow our heart and therefore we know that means we must let others in our society do the same. Let them follow their heart. We understand that trying to restrict another person from seeing someone else in any given capacity is not allowing that person to follow their heart. And thus, as "the one is the all, and the all are the one," we would simply not be allowing ourself to truly follow our heart!

Jefferson: That makes sense! That's how I've been trying to live my life, but in our society that is not accepted by all people.

Arvantis: We do not live in your society.

Jefferson: Sure...yeah, it makes sense. So...we have couples that get into an agreement that they will have a more serious relationship with each other. When do you get into such agreement? When both of your hearts say so?

Arvantis: What is a serious relationship?

Jefferson: No...just...serious in the sense that you are interacting with that person frequently on a daily basis and with greater intimacy.

Arvantis: It is something that simply occurs naturally, organically. We don't have to plan ahead for it.

Jefferson: What was the last game you played?

Arvantis: The last game I played?

Jefferson: Yes.

Arvantis: I don't recall having played a game recently.

Jefferson: What do you recall achieving recently with a group of people?

Arvantis: Achievement?

Jefferson: Yes.

Arvantis: What have we achieved lately?

Jefferson: Yes.

Arvantis: We are enjoying our world, our life, our interactions, and we are expanding our ability to communicate with realms and societies such as yours. It brings us great joy! That could be defined as an achievement, but again, we don't really define our world in terms of achieving something. We experience the joy of existence and follow our heart and in that way we are always able to experience what is uplifting for us. In that way we are being of greatest service to all that we are and to All That Is. And for us that is all the more achievement we have any designs on.

Jefferson: That is awesome! Okay, change of topic. What color is your tongue?

Arvantis: My tongue is rather reddish colored.

Jefferson: Hmm. Do you have an organ, as we do, called the heart?

Arvantis: We do!

Jefferson: Does it work the same way?

Arvantis: It has similar function.

Jefferson: And do you have nails?

Arvantis: I have something that is like a nail.

Jefferson: Do you have to clip?

Arvantis: There is no need for clipping, no.

Jefferson: How big is your foot?

Arvantis: My foot?

Jefferson: Yeah?

Arvantis: It is approximately fourteen of your inches from the back to the top tip of the toe.

Jefferson: Fourteen of our feet.

Arvantis: Inches.

Jefferson: Oh, okay, yes. Fourteen of our inches, yes. How big is your hand?

Arvantis: It is approximately five-and-a-half inches in the palm, from one side to the other.

Jefferson: Five and a half inches? My hand is bigger than that! My hand is eight inches!

Arvantis: Not counting the fingers. From one side of the palm to the other side of the palm.

Jefferson: Oh, okay...oh. It's just a little bit bigger than ours. And if you count the fingers?

Arvantis: Yes, we have four fingers.

Jefferson: No...if you count...you have four...you said you had five fingers?

Arvantis: If you count the thumb!

Jefferson: Okay. From the middle finger to the beginning of the hand, how big is it?

Arvantis: From the middle finger?

Jefferson: If you count the beginning of the hand to the end of the middle finger?

Arvantis: Yes. We're not clear on what you're asking…the beginning of the hand?

Jefferson: How big is your hand if you count the finger?

Arvantis: It's a big hand!

Jefferson: Okay!

Arvantis: For measurements, if you have a more specific question related to the measurements, perhaps we could provide you with a more clear answer.

Jefferson: I understand that the palm of your hand is five inches, but if you want to count the distance from the beginning of your hand to the tip of the finger, how big is that?

Arvantis: Approximately an additional four inches outward from the palm.

Jefferson: Okay, great, thank you. Now, what can you tell us today about your chin?

Arvantis: Our teeth?

Jefferson: Your chin.

Arvantis: Our chin?

Jefferson: Yes.

Arvantis: What would you like to know about our chin?

Jefferson: What does your chin look like? Does it look like mine?

Arvantis: It doesn't look that different!

Jefferson: Oh. Okay. And is there anyway you can elaborate on it?

Arvantis: Well, it has skin on it and underneath that there is a bone and that's about it!

Jefferson: So it's more protruding or...it doesn't stick out so much?

Arvantis: It doesn't stick out much. It's not something that protrudes outward very much.

Jefferson: Oh, okay. And, do you have whiskers?

Arvantis: Winters?

Jefferson: Whiskers.

Arvantis: Whiskers, no.

Jefferson: Oh, okay. And what is your nose like?

Arvantis: It's a little bit closer in to the face from what you generally find on your world. It doesn't stick out as far.

Jefferson: Hmm. And from the face to the tip of the nose, how big is it?

Arvantis: It depends on the size of the person you are talking to. Are you referring to or asking about me specifically?

Jefferson: Yes.

Arvantis: It is about an inch-and-a-half from the top to the base.

Jefferson: That's it? That is small! How cool! And as you grow older, does your nose continue to grow too?

Arvantis: It can, some.

Jefferson: Okay. Now, from the chin up, is your head a rectangular shape?

Arvantis: It is more oval shaped.

Jefferson: Like my head?

Arvantis: Yes.

Jefferson: Okay. So you are really close to the human in appearance right?

Arvantis: Not that much difference.

Jefferson: Now, if we were to measure from the tip of your chin to the top of your head, how long is that?

Arvantis: Approximately fourteen inches.

Jefferson: Oh fourteen inches. Okay. Now, in relationship to your digestive system, do you make trips to the toilet?

Arvantis: We do not have that need, no.

Jefferson: Oh, you dont? So in that case, you wouldn't have the digestion system that we have in our physiology for that use?

Arvantis: There are differences in our anatomy, yes.

Jefferson: There are differences? What difference?

Arvantis: That would be one!

Jefferson: Oh, that is something nice that you don't have to go to the toilet! Less time spent doing that.

Arvantis: Oh, you say you spend a lot of time there?

Jefferson: Well, sometimes when you have to go, you have to go, you know?

Arvantis: All right.

Jefferson: Do you have organs in your physiology that we don't have?

Arvantis: There are a few.

Jefferson: Talk to me about them, please.

Arvantis: We have an organ that digests what we ingest in a way that is different from what you have on your world. So we don't have the need for the elimination in the toilet that you have in your world. That is a primary diffence.

We have another organ that is in the cranial region of our brain that helps us to observe those beings in existences and realms that are of a different frequency than what you generally perceive in your life experience. In a sense, it makes us a little bit more intuitive, you might say, or have a greater sense of extra sensory perception.

Jefferson: Oh. With that particular organ, if you want to, you could close your eyes and see me here on Earth.

Arvantis: There are sometimes where that might work. Yes.

Jefferson: So it doesn't respond to your will? It works when it wants to?

Arvantis: There are times where the energies are more conducive to that type of application, and we are aware when those are in the most appropriate timing. We sense that and if we choose then we can simply utilize that timing for that type of activity, viewing.

Jefferson: Have you already seen me that way?

Arvantis: Yes.

Jefferson: When was the last time you did that?

Arvantis: That is something that will remain a mystery for quite some time.

Jefferson: Okay. Can you tell me...can you tell me about the organs that we don't have that you do?

Arvantis: There are those two...

Jefferson: Hey, by the way, that organ you just mentioned, is it in your brain or outside where people can see?

Arvantis: That would be in our brain region.

Jefferson: Would that be in the frontal lobe?

Arvantis: It is under the underside.

Jefferson: Where?

Arvantis: It is in the underside portion of our brain close to where our spine column comes up into the seat of the skull.

Jefferson: What other organs do you have that we don't?

Arvantis: For now, those two will suffice.

Jefferson: And do we, Earth humans, have any organs that you don't?

Arvantis: You do have a gallbladder and you do have your digestive tract of the large intestine, which is something that we do not have.

Jefferson: How about your female and male reproductive organs? Are they the same as in humans?

Arvantis: They aren't quite the same, but there are some similarities.

Jefferson: And are they external?

Arvantis: There is some external quality, primarily with the male features.

Jefferson: Do you pee...urinate?

Arvantis: That is something that our other organ related to our digestive system takes care of.

Jefferson: Can you explain to me the process of producing offspring?

Arvantis: It isn't that different from in your world.

Jefferson: Okay. Do you guys tell jokes?

Arvantis: No. We have a great deal of fun, and humor, but there are no real jokes, in that sense.

Jefferson: Do you play any musical instrument?

Arvantis: I don't. There are those who play instruments, you could call them. They have sounds of a musical quality.

Jefferson: Hmm. Do you consider yourself a scientist?

Arvantis: I am.

Jefferson: And since you made the amulet that you have, could we consider you a carpenter?

Arvantis: That would not make me a carpenter.

Jefferson: What would that make you?

Arvantis: Someone who is following their heart, designing, creating something that is of great joy and pleasure.

Jefferson: When you go to school, do you take notebooks or only mental notes?

Arvantis: We do not have a school system as you have in your world.

Jefferson: So you learn by experience?

Arvantis: Primarily, yes. There are times that we will sit down in groups and those who have something that they are in greatest joy to learn, will have it presented to them by someone who is of greatest joy to share that information with them.

Jefferson: So education in these groups is based more on an individual's excitement rather than a program that is pre-chosen?

Arvantis: They do not have to follow a curriculum as you have in your school systems.

Jefferson: Thanks. Do you pray to God?

Arvantis: Could you define that?

Jefferson: God is...you are doing this on purpose right? Okay. God is a being, an external entity that can bless you if you pray to him?

Arvantis: Who is he again?

Jefferson: God is someone that we name as the Creator of everything!

Arvantis: Where does he live again?

Jefferson: He lives in...well...do you want me to tell you my version or a general version?

Arvantis: As you wish.

Jefferson: A general version is that he lives somewhere above the sky, somewhere in heaven. And that he has many people there, like angels and saints, and when you pray to him you get what you want!

Arvantis: Very well. So do you have all you want, or haven't you been praying?

Jefferson: Yeah, everything. Everyday I have everything that I ask for. (Laughter).

Arvantis: Very good, you must pray a lot.

Jefferson: No, I don't pray that way! But do you guys...obviously you don't pray in that way, to an external god, because you know everybody is part of God, within us all.

Arvantis: That is more like it.

Jefferson: Do you know of any civilization that prays to an external god?

Arvantis: Yours.

Jefferson: Is there another one?

Arvantis: Not to the degree that your society has developed.

Jefferson: Are there memories of your childhood that were fun for you that you would like to share with me?

Arvantis: Well, to your prior question, there may be other societies who are like yours in "praying to an external god." But in our awareness, yours is the only one that we know of. Certainly there could be others that we simply haven't become aware of.
To your current question, there is not presently any childhood idea of memories that come to mind, but thank you for the question!

Jefferson: How quick can you run?

Arvantis: I move approximately thirty kilometers-per-hour.

Jefferson: Running?

Arvantis: Yes.

Jefferson: Can your brother beat you?

Arvantis: That isn't something that would be in our mind.

Jefferson: No, I mean running faster!

Arvantis: I don't know.

Jefferson: Can you tell me something that you remember very clearly that your dad or your mom taught you?

Arvantis: They both have been great gifts and guides in every moment of my interaction with them. So then there is no one thing that stands out among the others.

Jefferson: Is there anything that comes to mind that your brother taught you?

Arvantis: There are continuous opportunities in all interactions with the people on our world to learn new things. It is something that we simply allow to happen without trying to identify it as being something that we learned from that person or this person. We simply allow for the experiences and growth processes in our interactions with others to come and go without archiving them, without trying to put them in filing systems of who taught me this and who taught me that.

Jefferson: Okay. Your brother is twelve years old. How tall is he?

Arvantis: He is approximately 7.2 feet tall.

Jefferson: He is taller than you?

Arvantis: If you say so.

Jefferson: Remember, you told me that you were 6.5 feet and that in five years you would be 7.5 feet?

Arvantis: That time has yet to come.

Jefferson: So how tall are you today?

Arvantis: Approximately 6.5 feet.

Jefferson: Your brother is taller than you?

Arvantis: If you say so.

Jefferson: I thought he was smaller than you?

Arvantis: Not at this timing.

Jefferson: In regards to the idea of a consciousness exchange. Since we are both the same soul, could we have a consciousness exchange where you become aware of yourself as me and I become aware of myself as you? How could we go about doing that?

Arvantis: There is simply the desire to do that, to make the connection and communication to develop that frequency of similarity.

Jefferson: Okay.

Arvantis: It is something that, over time, you could develop.

Jefferson: Well...basically it could be almost like in the movie "K-Pax." There is a movie in our world called "K-Pax." The guy is almost like a channel by being a few days in the body of another person. Do you understand that this is what I mean?

Arvantis: A walk-in?

Jefferson: Yeah, almost like a walk-in, but later on you go back to your Arvantis body and I come back to my Jefferson body!

Arvantis: A walk out!

Jefferson: (Laughter). So that is possible, right?

Arvantis: Yes.

Jefferson: Hey Arvantis, do you have shamans in your world?

Arvantis: No.

Jefferson: No shamans. Do you have the "wise" people?

Arvantis: There are those who have particular areas of focus that are of great intelligence in that field.

Jefferson: Have you ever gone to any of them for any question?

Arvantis: It happens, sure.

Jefferson: Can you share the last time that you went there?

Arvantis: Nothing comes to mind.

Jefferson: Oh. Is there anything we can do at some point to talk to one of them so they can teach your ways of knowledge in that particular field.

Arvantis: We might be able to bridge that type of interaction and have that form of interaction take place through the words in this fashion. If you had particular questions of something of that nature, I might be able to talk with one at another timing, at another channeling session.

Jefferson: Yes, sure, but not in this particular moment. We are running out of time now. There are other things I want to talk to you about. What is your moms name?

Arvantis: That isn't available at this timing.

Jefferson: Let me ask you something else. You said you appreciate the playful way your brother has to teach people.

Arvantis: Yes.

Jefferson: Can you tell your brother, through telepathy now, to tell us a unique quality that he sees you express that he appreciates in you?

Arvantis: Not at this timing.

Jefferson: Why is that?

Arvantis: It's simply not a form of discussion or interaction available at this present timing.

Jefferson: Where is your girlfriend located at this time?

Arvantis: There are girls here who are friends of mine. The one I have contact with most regularly is presently on another region of the surface of our planet. She is exploring various ideas with a few other people of our society as well.

Jefferson: Is she a scientist too?

Arvantis: That is something that she could be labeled in that capacity, but we don't think of ourselves as scientists in quite the same way that you generally have on your world.

Jefferson: I have heard that Feline races are known to be master geneticists. Can you comment on that?

Arvantis: There are some within our society who have a talent and a joy working with genetics, but how —

Jefferson: Are you able to clone an Arkoreun?

Arvantis: We have the ability to make such an adjustment in physiology, yes.

Jefferson: Are you saying that you can have an Arkoreun come to life without having it happen through the birth canal and the reproduction process we have?

Arvantis: It is quite a complex process to bring that into a reality.

Jefferson: So you don't do that?

Arvantis: It is something that has occured at times, but it is something that we don't do very frequently.

Jefferson: What were you doing before this session?

Arvantis: I was having a drink of some air, a very delicious oxygen.

Taking it in and feeling my life force with a sense of joy for approximately what you would think of as a half-an-hour of your time.

Jefferson: Could we say that you were meditating?

Arvantis: There could be that, yes. But then I was very active in interacting with the environment, the outdoor environment around me that I was resting and sitting within.

Jefferson: How many hours do you sleep?

Arvantis: It varies. Approximtely one-and-a-half to three hours, but that can be altered. We can, and I can, go a few days of the Sun's passage through our skies without sleeping. But generally I won't do that.

Jefferson: From your waist to the bottom of your feet, how long is that?

Arvantis: Aproximately four feet.

Jefferson: Is there a question that I may not have asked that you would like to share with us today?

Arvantis: No. We are wonderful in this interaction with you!

Jefferson: Is there anyone around there that would like to ask a question?

Arvantis: Not at this timing, but thank you for asking!

Jefferson: Fantastic! So what are you up to now?

Arvantis: I suppose we will continue with our drinking in of some more oxygen. Enjoying the flavor of the sky.

Jefferson: And whatever comes next, will come next.

Arvantis: And you? What will you be doing next?

Jefferson: Ah, I guess I will have dinner and then sleep.

Arvantis: Very well.

Jefferson: Hey, have I been to your planet in a dream state any of these days?

Arvantis: There may have been that visitation, but we will leave that to you.

Jefferson: And you haven't physically been here, lately?

Arvantis: Not the physical.

Jefferson: Okay, well, then I say, wonderful prints of paws and purring to swim within your heart this day of our time!

Arvantis: Oh, wonderful! Thank you for that kind, playful, sharing of words. We look forward to our next engagement in this format with you of communicating and exploring. Allow yourself to live your life each moment as best you can, as you feel most inclined to. Let it be joyful, if you will, for there is much joy for you in the lands you reside in today.

Jefferson: Sure, fantastic! Once again, thank you and I will talk to you soon!

Arvantis: Yes, until then, live your life upliftingly and let the soul and the Sun within your heart illuminate outward and nourish you and those in your presence as well, frequently and warmingly as you will. Thank you dear one. Until we are together in this way again, good fantastic journeys with you!

Jefferson: Thank you very much Arvantis, bye!

Chapter 7

How To Be of Greatest Service To Others

"When you follow your heart in each moment, you are being of greatest service to All That Is as best you can be in your current physical incarnation."

- Arvantis

February 9th, 2010

Arvantis: Wonderful to be in this interchange of communication with soul reflection in this avenue, in this way, in this form, in this world of physical creation together in this moment of our timing together. How are you there Jefferson?

Jefferson: It's adorable to have the opportunity to speak to you!

Arvantis: Lovely, you as well!

Jefferson: It's wonderful to be able to have access to the basics in life. I really want to have the opportunity to give all that I have to, you know, give everyone else the opportunity to have all that I have. When do you think that is going to happen?

Arvantis: When you are following your heart, then you are doing just that. In each moment then, you are providing in all of the ways that you can for all who are there, all who exist, and you are doing so in the best way possible when you follow your heart. It really is that simple. You don't have to make it complicated or complex. You don't have to require yourself to achieve or accomplish an enormous amount of activities. So it can be very simple!

Jefferson: What are the initial thoughts you want to share with us at the beginning of this chapter?

Arvantis: We will allow you then to move forward with the theme for this chapter in whatever fashion you feel most inclined, nudged, excited, joyed, to do.

Jefferson: Thank you! I have just a few questions I probably didn't go through in the other chapters with you, so I will touch on them quickly. About your eyes, what society is responsible for your eyes being further out on the surface of the face, rather than set in some like ours are?

Arvantis: That is simply something genetically that has occurred over time. You could call it evolution, but there has been some creation, some genetic alterations to have some adjustments made in those locations. So it's something that happened, in terms of your sense of time – past, present and future – it is something that has happened over a period of thousands of years as you keep track of time. Over thousands, upon thousands, upon thousands, upon thousands of your years this process has developed.

There are numerous life forms that would be humanoid, similar to yours, but with variations such as you speak of like the eyes that exist. Given all of these variations that are available to choose from, if one wants then to create a new genetic form, a new humanoid form, there is then all of those existing humanoid forms from which to draw from genetically and to then thus create a new life form. Somewhat similar to how you have on your world alterations of various forms of foods, and fruits, and flowers. Creating new life forms from existing forms.

Jefferson: So basically, a physical life-form will adapt to the environment it is exposed to?

Arvantis: There is some of that, but there are also environments that are found to be suitable for a particular life experience and life exploration. When a physical life-form is going to be designed for a life space, a planetary region, it will be designed to be, in a sense, set up to be adapted before it is even created. So that life-form will have all the adaptations already built-in to its biology before it is even placed into that planetary environment.

Jefferson: Thank you! Previously I asked you, "How big are your eyes?" You said they're big! I found that to be fun! What is the size from one side of your eyes to the other?

Arvantis: Somewhat wider than your eyes.

Jefferson: Do they sit on your face like my eyes sit on mine...in a horizontal line?

Arvantis: The portion of the eyes that are closest to our ears are generally up higher than you would find on most of the humans on your world at this timing.

Jefferson: Oh! I see. And do you have the tear duct?

Arvantis: That is something that does exist.

Jefferson: And what about lips? Do you have lips?

Arvantis: Yes, we do.

Jefferson: And is it on you like it is on me?

Arvantis: There are some similarities, yes. There is a region just below the nose that on your world often has a bit of a dimple effect in the center of the upper lip, and that generally is something we won't find with ours. It isn't something that commonly occurs in our biology, that dimple effect. With Earth human lips, there are a couple of soft ridges that, in a sense, come down directly below the openings of the nostrils of the nose and there is a soft depression of the skin between those two ridges. That dimple then is something that often in our biology you won't find that.

Jefferson: And do you have the belly button?

Arvantis: No, that is something that we do not have. Generally our skin adapts after birth so that is something that becomes very soft and smooth and blends in with the surrounding skin in that region so that there isn't really a depression in that way that you call a belly button in your world.

Jefferson: How many months do pre-borns stay in their mom's womb?

Arvantis: Generally seven months with four months additional at times. The seven months would be the earliest you would find birthing and then there could be an additional four month period that could occur in the mother's womb in the embryonic state, in the development state, the gestation period, the growth period. This provides an accumulative time of eleven months for those pre-born beings that use the additional four months before birth.

Jefferson: Oh, I see. What about Arvantis? How long did he take to be born?

Arvantis: Approximately eleven!

Jefferson: Why did you take the extra four?

Arvantis: There was some period there of development taking place with the mother. In that sense, communications were occurring that were giving this then embryo, this unborn being, the opportunity to grow and become aware in ways that often a seven month birthing being would not have access to. It was a bit of a four month education, in a sense, that takes place while still being in the mother and having a more direct contact with the mother.

This provides the mother with a new experience and some more deepening of understanding of the birthing process and what a being within the physiology of the mother is capable of developing into at that state, capable of learning at that state, in terms of what it is going through while in the womb. Thus this mother is then able to teach future mothers-to-be more about what the birthing process can be like in the development stages.

So then, new mothers-to-be can be more affectionate towards the growing embryo at the early stages, at the one month stage, the two month stage, the three month stage, and so on until birth. In that way the mother to-be can be more affectionate towards the yet to-be born child within them, can find new ways to connect and be more at-one with this yet to-be born life-form within them. Do you follow? Do you understand? Does that provide you with some clarity?

Jefferson: Yes. You said your skin is light blue. Do you have...tiger stripes or any marks like that?

Arvantis: We would not appear to be a striped person, no!

Jefferson: But do you have anything like it...or is the skin just light blue all over and that's it?

Arvantis: There are some variations, some spots here and there that occur upon the skin surface for various reasons that are not necessarily something we have chosen in our aware state of being that we could say, this is that way because of this! It is something that just occurs, in a sense, to the growth and development of our skin, of our biology, of our bodily being.

Jefferson: So are you speaking of birth marks?

Arvantis: There are some things that could exist at birth, in that sense, some spots, some variations in color. But as we develop and grow, there are changes that can occur and spots that can grow and appear that weren't there at birth. Some spots that were there at birth can, in a sense, disappear over time.

Jefferson: Do you have any?

Arvantis: I do have a few but nothing that would be remarkable or noticeable.

Jefferson: Oh, okay. What about the pants you said you wear? Are you wearing them now?

Arvantis: I do have some clothing on that is of an organic fabric. It has, in a sense, a cloth quality that is very similar to plants that we have on this world, and a bit like the fibrous sheathing on trees. It's kind of a combination. It's a bit more flexible than you would find bark on a tree to be and a bit more durable and stronger than you would find the large leaves of the plants to have.

Jefferson: You said you don't usually change pants or shirts, and that they clean their self. Are you wearing the same ones as before?

Arvantis: I have some clothing on that was with me the last time we spoke.

Jefferson: I see. But it's not the same that you wear your entire life?

Arvantis: I do have some options. So I am not always wearing the same ones throughout my life.

Jefferson: Okay. Where do you put the one you don't want to wear anymore?

Arvantis: When I sense that I don't want to wear something anymore, then I have a way in which we do of letting it go where it can, in a sense, resolve itself back into nature, change its shape and form and become one with the ground, the substance of matter of the planet that we live upon.

Jefferson: When you said your hair and shirt take care of themselves, does it mean you impose your will over the matter or that the matter is conscious and agrees to serve you in that way?

Arvantis: It has a natural and built-in ability to be self-cleaning in that way, in that sense. We don't have to consciously apply ideas of cleaning it.

Jefferson: Do you wear on your head or on your face an artwork that you manually do?

Arvantis: An artwork?

Jefferson: Yeah!

Arvantis: We do have some items that occasionally we place around.

They are a bit like what you would call a necklace and a pendant. Usually they are a symbol of our existence, our interaction with those before us, and our interaction with nature. They aren't just a way of decorating ourselves for the sake of fashion.

Jefferson: Do you kiss one another like we do or is there more of an energetic exchange of feelings?

Arvantis: We do have both, this occurs both ways.

Jefferson: Oh, I see! When was your first interaction with Earth?

Arvantis: That was something that I had at a very young age, approximately fifteen, the fifteenth orbit around my Sun.

Jefferson: I don't understand?

Arvantis: You would consider it to be a —

Jefferson: I thought you viewed some historic records and saw me when you were at the age of five. So I understand that to be the first visual contact you had with me in this lifetime, right?

Arvantis: Yes. And my first interaction with Earth was when I was fifteen.

Jefferson: Oh, okay. When was the first contact that your race had with Earth?

Arvantis: That is something that occurred many, many eons ago in terms of our ability to be aware of Earth, to be able to understand it as a planet that has life on it.

Jefferson: I see.

Arvantis: So this occurred well before my physical incarnation on the planet.

Jefferson: Can you tell me more about that...your physical incarnation on the planet as me or as who?

Arvantis: As my present incarnation. Our society has been aware of your world and existence well before I was born in this current incarnation.

Jefferson: And do you know how it happened or what caused your world to become aware of Earth?

Arvantis: There were explorers that were mapping the cosmos for their records. They were visiting our society. They provided us, in exchange for some of our information, those portions of their mapping that contained the information with the knowledge of your existence and your planet. There were various timelines of life on Earth that they were able to record and document, in that sense, in a way you would be able to understand the idea of archiving information.

Jefferson: And the first time that you came to Earth was when you visited me?

Arvantis: That was the first time that I was able to be in the presence of other Earth humans that are of the current era, similar to that which you are a part of with the dynamics that exist on your world, the focus of belief systems, the focus of what you are and who you are. In that sense, these things are like an era, a chapter in a book. For there have been many other life forms on Earth. Of those, some are human and had very different belief structures than that which you have in your era. They then would be considered a different era, a different chapter.

Jefferson: Okay.

Arvantis: I have visited Earth in some of those other eras as well to give me more of an idea of what it is like on Earth from different timeframes that have different belief system structures.

Jefferson: Yeah.

Arvantis: It provides me with some background and some frame of reference in interacting with you in your era, in your society's current collective consciousness.

Jefferson: And just so our readers and I can understand, what were you referring to earlier when you brought up the number fifteen?

Arvantis: That relates to the timing of my existence on my planet as it made its fifteenth orbit around its Sun, when I began my initial physical interaction with your planet.

Jefferson: Oh.

Arvantis: In a timeframe that was of another era, not of the one you currently are in. The one you're in, in our understanding, your current era began approximately within the 230,000 year ago time-cycle.

Jefferson: Okay.

Arvantis: I have visited other eras before and after that era. My first visitation physically was in an entirely different era in which you were not there and the collective consciousness structure you have today was not present there at all.

Jefferson: So you can go back in time? You can time travel?

Arvantis: As you understand the idea of past, present, and future, I can move into different realities that define themselves as being in a particular timeline and that could be called a time travel. But to me, it seems like I am in the present time no matter what timeline those who are around me are defining themselves to be in. I do not have the sense that I am in the past. If I appear in a society that is saying that they are in the past relative to what you would call the past, I do not feel as though I am in the past. I always feel as though I am in the present.

Jefferson: Hmm...if you wanted to come back and visit me when I am at a different age, could you do that?

Arvantis: There is some possibility for that to occur, a different timeline, a different parallel reality, yes that can occur! For actually I am on all of those timeframes, but then, only the ones that are pertinent to the conversation in any given moment that I am interacting with you will be the ones that I will be accessing.

Jefferson: Sure!

Arvantis: And there can be changes in information of this nature that you are asking. You might think you are asking me questions and collecting facts that do not change and therefore are static, but in terms of the nature of existence, these things do change and are not actually static, they do change. So there can be changes in these answers that relate to these questions that you ask.

It can be a little bit challenging for those on your world to make the adjustment, to begin asking and gathering information that is more in alignment with the actual ever-changing nature of your existence and that allow you to then spend your time, as you perceive spending time, in ways that will provide you with such information that can be more supportive for your experiences in each moment. After you make this adjustment, things that you once wrote down as a fact, as a recorded documented fact, won't be as important to you anymore because you will begin to realize that many such facts can change. Even how you perceive them can change.

Jefferson: Okay.

Arvantis: And then you can approach those ideas in a more flexible and less intense manner, without the idea of thinking that they are going to provide you with a background that will then give you a framework from which to always access and experience life through and from, as though they could symbolically provide you with a house in which the walls are always in the same place and the doors are always in the same place.

We understand how fact gathering can provide you with comfort, with a sense of security, but the nature of things are always changing. Even walls in a house are always really changing, and so then as you move to accept this understanding that the walls of the very homes that you live in can then thus begin changing their locations and the doors and windows can begin changing their location, it makes it easier for you to move things about, to move to different geographical regions a little bit more easily. For you will be able to construct homes more readily. That then will afford you the ability to move about more freely and not be tied down to concrete foundations, as if they were facts that could not be altered once they were set and recorded, cast in concrete, cast in stone.

Realizing how things are always changing will also provide your society more acceptance in the idea that they don't have to be tied down to house mortgages, and home payments, and a job that they currently perceive will provide them with money to make the payments for the mortgages that they perceive they have to have if they are going to have a home.

As the ability to move about more freely in the ever changing reality becomes more understood in your world, as you learn to access that ability within you more readily, then there is no need to cast concrete foundations and to have mortgage systems that require you to make monthly payments, that require you thus then to have jobs in order to have the money to make those payments.

It can support your growth to let go of the idea that facts are unchanging, that facts are really important to jot down, and to record, and to categorize, and to label, and to create volumes and volumes and volumes and volumes and volumes of records and folders and file cabinets filled with facts and books, and books filled with facts as if they were then going to be the foundation of all future experiences for you to build upon. That type of activity is only casting yourself into a home that seems to have a concrete foundation and immovable walls, in terms of how you experience your reality.

Let the facts go and you will no longer need to be making payments for a mortgage on a house. You will be able to move about more flexibly and be where you need to be when you need to be there. And live where it is most appropriate and joyful for you to live when you want to live there. You won't have to work in a job in order to make money to make the payments, for you will not have anything you need to pay. You will not have any obligations. You will simply be allowing yourself to be in alignment more with your actual nature. We understand your focus on facts, but begin to allow yourself to realize they really don't allow you to be the flexible, ever changing dynamic aspect of existence that you truly are, and they won't always provide you with a sense of experiencing your actual existence in the ways you presently perhaps think they can. So we perceive it is a big shift for you to focus less on facts, but it will be a valuable one to begin allowing yourself to consider doing so, at the pace and the timing that is appropriate for you and for each of you.

Jefferson: Okay, sure, I see. Would it be possible for you to go to that timeline when I was fifteen and educate me more about you so

when I am twenty-nine I will be fully aware of your existence and able to teach people of our meetings and travels to other worlds?

Arvantis: You can do that! With your intention, spend time focusing on connecting to those experiences, those interchanges, that reality, and then it will begin. Information, experiences, knowledge, abilities, skill, talents from those interactions will begin to come through for you. As they do, you might not recognize them as coming from those interactions, but it is what would be occurring for you.

The more you choose to sit down and meditate on that connection taking place, know then that it is. Don't question it. Allow it to be so for you. Before you go to sleep, you can ask that it happen in your dreamtime as well. This can function in such a way that you might actually begin to have the experience of the interchange taking place, as though it was a real experience for you, as though you were aware of it actually taking place, human to human, person to person! It can occur in that way too, but again, meditating on it, giving yourself time for the interchange to take place with a mind at rest, without thinking or wondering if it is happening, have the intent for it to happen. Then give time, peaceful time, quiet time, for it to occur, as though it is like a silent download from a computer, from a file being downloaded onto your computer. Let it happen that way as well. Then give time for the information that you download to begin to reveal itself for you. To speed up the opportunities that come before you so you can then act in these ways that you have suggested you would like to move forward in within your physical reality. Do you follow this idea?

Jefferson: So with intention, imagination, and true sincere desire, I can change the past?

Arvantis: And taking action, doing, doing, doing it! Doing the meditation, having the intent before you go to sleep to have such experiences in your dreamtime. Do. Have the intent and then do. Act in this way. Give it time to grow as if you were planting a seed and then you are nourishing it with water and sunlight. Give it time to grow and take time to rest, to sit, to be still, to let the seed germinate, to let the download transfer the information fully. That then the sprout of knowledge can surface above the soil of your previously unseen world of your subconscious into your aware conscience.

Jefferson: Lovely, thank you! So when I change the past, it will have an effect on the present?

Arvantis: In ways you perhaps will not know happened because then you would not have lived that other present.

Jefferson: That's really powerful, huh?

Arvantis: It is.

Jefferson: Have I ever told you, you are very funny?

Arvantis: You have.

Jefferson: I have? When? When you were here physically?

Arvantis: We hear you talk in your sleep.

Jefferson: You do?

Arvantis: Yes!

Jefferson: Oh, tell me the last time this happened?

Arvantis: Not recently, but we have heard you say it before.

Jefferson: Oh! I see, okay. Do you wear gloves?

Arvantis: I do not.

Jefferson: Have you ever worn one?

Arvantis: I have.

Jefferson: What for?

Arvantis: For the fun of it.

Jefferson: Nah, seriously?

Arvantis: I found it quite exciting.

Jefferson: Where?

Arvantis: On my hands.

Jefferson: No, no, but on what planet?

Arvantis: There have been a few occasions, even on your world, to try on a glove.

Jefferson: Okay. What can you tell me today about what people call the Akashic Records?

Arvantis: What would you like to know?

Jefferson: Is that Akashic a living being like a craft, like a planet, or just a self- containing matrix system?

Arvantis: There is both.

Jefferson: Oh, okay. Now, is it true that after we die, after our body dies, we don't cease to exist?

Arvantis: You will continue to exist in some way.

Jefferson: And is that way pertaining to the person's future choices or...

Arvantis: Yes!

Jefferson: And also, more on wanting to educate ourselves about this idea of life after death, I would like to have some illustration. So can you please go with me to the last time I died and tell me what happened?

Arvantis: There were — in this incarnation that we will speak of, not your most recent one — there was in another lifetime the transfer out of your biology into a spacious awareness of the world you had just departed from. You then had the ability to see it as though you were another person visually observing the body you had just transitioned out of. There were others in the world you departed that you could interact with, but they couldn't see or hear you. The interaction you had was in a very subtle way.

The people you interacted with had a very soft sense that you were closer to them somehow, as though you were communicating to them from the other side. They weren't aware what you were saying. They just felt your presence in a different way because they could see you were not animating the physical body you had transitioned out of. They were aware you had passed on, but they felt somehow you were closer to them in a different way. They sensed that must be your spirit talking and being with them.

You were there, softly stroking their hair. You were softly moving your hand through their hair and softly caressing their shoulder, softly whispering in their ear delicate words of gratitude, of love, and all that you appreciated about them that you hadn't conveyed to them while in physical bodily form. For you, it was like you were still in that just departed world, but you felt they couldn't quite connect with you.

Jefferson: Okay.

Arvantis: So it was a bit like you were an invisible man, in that sense, and that was a little bit disconcerting, but you quickly made the adjustment by understanding what had occurred. You were able to accept it. You had a sensing that you were going to be moving forward in a way that would be appropriate for you. You had a sensing that it was all going to be very well for you in a way that felt uplifting, that felt nurturing for you.

Jefferson: Interesting!

Arvantis: There was still a slight sense that you would have liked to have been able to have a more direct communication with those who you had, in a sense, departed from. You shared with them as well as you could, which was a very rich form of communication, and sharing, and loving that you had towards those beings that were part of a family. This then would not have been your most recent lifetime before your present embodiment, but it would have been approximately three lifetimes prior to your current lifetime that we are referring to when we speak of this transition out of that lifetime.

Jefferson: And what about the last lifetime I departed?

Arvantis: That is not in this timing available for us, for any number of reasons, to bring forth any information for you about.

Jefferson: And this one that you brought up was around what year?

Arvantis: For you it would have been in the 1700's, approximately 1715 to 1750.

Jefferson: Okay. Very good, Can you tell us a little bit about what happened to the Giordano Bruno life that I had, right after I left the body?

Arvantis: That then, in this timing, will only suffice to say that it wasn't like what we just spoke of.

Jefferson: Okay.

Arvantis: It was a little bit different for various reasons and that then eventually brought you to a different experience when you made that transition. We will at another time — if you ask the question again and depending on the timing — be able to provide you with more. At this timing, the one lifetime we shared with you...we would like that to percolate with you for a few of your days first.

Jefferson: And what was I in the lifetime that you just shared with me?

Arvantis: That then is not the focus for now. We feel the information we've given is the most important to percolate within you for now.

Jefferson: Yeah, I sort of had some images as you were saying...

Arvantis: Very good, yes! Thank you for sharing!

Jefferson: When was the last time you died?

Arvantis: That is something that would have been for me... I don't recount.

Jefferson: And do you remember where you went?

Arvantis: I do not.

Jefferson: Can an Arkoreun know the day of his or her death?

Arvantis: Yes.

Jefferson: You can?

Arvantis: Sure!

Jefferson: Oh, because you choose the day you are going to die?

Arvantis: There are those who are aware of this and then there are those gatherings to honor that transition before the actual transition takes place amongst those who are closest in their interactions with such a person that has chosen to make such a transition. You could call it a going away party!

Jefferson: Can you know the dates a human like myself will make the transition?

Arvantis: There are sometimes where this can be observed ahead of time, but generally it is not something we apply our awareness to receiving.

Jefferson: Tell me something, just out of the blue!

Arvantis: Yes, out of the blue comes a bright, bright cloud filled with flowers of comfort and effervescence for you to play in, to swim in, out of the blue for you this moment of our time together, as you asked.

Jefferson: I also feel strongly connected with the idea of the Andromeda Star System. Since I was a little kid, whenever I heard that name, some unexplainable feelings of peace, joy, adventure,

and passion would erupt within me. Can you tell me why that is?

Arvantis: There is a very close connection you have with this time, place, existence, and quality of energies that are of you that you refer to as the Andromeda. There is then a whole society there of which you have been a part of, currently are a part of, and they then know that you are living in this lifetime, coexisting on this planet of physiological life forms, in that sense. Having a physical experience in two entirely different planets. So there is then, in that sense, a very strong connection you have with that other you on that world in this timing.

Jefferson: As I am speaking to you, it feels like I am passionate about that idea for some reason?!

Arvantis: Very good!

Jefferson: So you said that I am currently living a lifetime in two different planets of the Andromeda system?

Arvantis: There are two lifetimes coexisting. One in the Andromeda system and this one that you have here.

Jefferson: In the Arkoreuns?

Arvantis: The physical one that you have that is asking the questions now.

Jefferson: Okay. Then we are three! Him, you, and me!

Arvantis: You can look at it that way, yes!

Jefferson: And how old is he?

Arvantis: That is information not available at this timing.

Jefferson: What then...wow! What else can you tell me...briefly about him or his world? Have you met him?

Arvantis: I am not aware of having met this individual, no. There are the energies there, very strong and supporting the idea of upliftment, and letting go of the sense that exists in your world of being separate. So that world and that individual has a strong energy, exciting, very deep excitement to provide that which then would assist you in moving through the constructs of limitation, the belief systems that are of limiting quality and definitions.

Jefferson: Wow! And what planet is that?

Arvantis: That is information not available either at this timing for any number of reasons which we are not presently aware of.

Jefferson: Wow, so now I understand why I...since the first time I heard that word and felt the way I felt. I am, as you said, strongly connected with that being?

Arvantis: Yes!

Jefferson: Wow, isn't this exciting?

Arvantis: Yes!

Jefferson: Wow. Hey, is it true that all human life originated on Lyra?

Arvantis: Well, that isn't something we would consider to be accurate when considering humans can exist in a multitude of different locations. But there is in your current timeframe the ability to create the idea, as it connects to your current era of collective consciousness, the idea that there was a beginning point. You can create the idea of that being on Lyra. There are those who do, but again, you have always existed and you exist in all those other planetary quadrants within an infinite number of physical universes.

Jefferson: Many extraterrestrial teachers speak of Earth as a third density planet. How many creational dimensions are there? Is it eleven?

Arvantis: There is as many as you like.

Jefferson: Right?! No, but in the sense that we speak of that Earth is on the third dimension. What would that make you and your society?

Arvantis: We generally don't interact in that way, but we understand you have the desire to define yourself in a dimensional sense, so there are in your world some of us who would be considered to be of a fifth dimensional to sixth dimensional consciousness.

Jefferson: I have heard that fifth dimensional beings can teleport themselves and that they have many other perks!

Arvantis: Many other ports?

Jefferson: No, perks, p, e, r, k.

Arvantis: Perks?

Jefferson: Yeah, you know…many other good things that come within the package of fifth density.

Arvantis: Well, if you aren't prepared for it then it could be quite painful.

Jefferson: Oh, yeah…okay! Have you ever teleported yourself?

Arvantis: I have had the experience through others.

Jefferson: But with a machine or just with your desire?

Arvantis: I have not within the sense of using a machine. That would be a bit of a frequency not to my preference.

Jefferson: So you teleported yourself already?

Arvantis: There is something you could call teleporting. Simply move about from one place to another through a focus of frequency.

Jefferson: Yeah. How do you do that?

Arvantis: How don't you do that?

Jefferson: I know, right?

Arvantis: Something we have grown with, born with, understand. It is like breathing. We know how to do it. It's just natural for us.

Jefferson: And what other abilities like that do you express that exceed Earth humans?

Arvantis: Well, we have a variety of modes and functions that wouldn't be in your world considered possible. There is that idea of moving about freely. There are any number of others too. We live with a different type of nourishment, and so food as you eat it isn't something that we go through with such a regular basis.

Jefferson: Yes! Hmm. And can you create houses out of your heart's desire?

Arvantis: We work with the various forms of organic life that live here on the planet. Some are almost naturally designed as abodes, as homes. They naturally provide us with shelter if we feel that we need that. But generally on our world, we can just exist on the surface without the need to inhabit a house like you have there.

Jefferson: Oh, I see. Does it rain?

Arvantis: We do have some moisture that comes through. A little bit differently than falling from the sky. It tends to just manifest in the space, in our air, as it were. And that is a form of rain for us. It brings moisture or water to the planet. Our planet has quite a bit of water and rivers on it already that are self-sustaining, capable of sustaining themselves without the need for the idea of rain to fall from the sky above.

Jefferson: Okay.

Arvantis: It is able to manifest this water molecule. This water is somewhat different than your water molecule. In our world, it is able to manifest and to, in a sense, sustain itself continuously. It changes its function to some degree, but it doesn't evaporate into another form as you find water drying up on your world.

Jefferson: I see.

Arvantis: On our world, it tends to maintain its fluid water quality and so we don't really need water to be falling from the sky to seemingly replenish the supply.

Jefferson: I missed a question that I was intending to ask when you spoke about time travel. If you can time travel, you already know what happened to Earth in 2012?

Arvantis: Well, we do know of things that have occurred on different Earths that do exist. There is more than one Earth at 2012. Which one will your society choose, in terms of how you perceive choice, which Earth 2012 will your society choose to manifest, to be connected to in terms of that frequency of that physical reality. Which one will you be choosing and perceive yourself to have chosen when that time is upon you, for there is more than one version of Earth at 2012, as we said.

Jefferson: How many?

Arvantis: We don't necessarily see all of them, but we do see more then one!

Jefferson: And can you speak a little bit about the most prominent one?

Arvantis: Well then, it is something that we can talk about ever briefly. There is still a world as you have today, in that sense, the land, the people, the communication systems as you still have today. It won't be that different in those types of structures.

Jefferson: But in relationship to our awareness of extraterrestrial existence?

Arvantis: In our perception, there will be more people at that timeline that will be open to the idea that ETs exist. This being the version of Earth that your personality will most likely be tuned to at 2012.

Jefferson: Where is the postcard at this timing?

Arvantis: That then will appear in appropriate timing as well.

Jefferson: Is it already in our solar system?

Arvantis: Yes.

Jefferson: Nice! And how did it get here?

Arvantis: We were working on it.

Jefferson: Great. Wow! Do you have any parting thoughts? It's about time to say goodbye for now.

Arvantis: "Goodbye for now." Well, we are all here, present and grateful for the interaction with you. We are very appreciative of the choice you have made to interact with us, to take time and write down questions and go through the process of exploring within your own imagination and sense of life experience what more you would like to know about us. We take great joy in your willingness to move forth in these ways, to focus your efforts in these ways. We sense for you it is a joy to do so!

Jefferson: Yes!

Arvantis: Thank you! Much Joy!

Jefferson: Wonderful prints of paws and purrings to swim within your heart!

Arvantis: Lovely! Thank you.

Jefferson: So any chance you can briefly tell us about your surroundings?

Arvantis: I am in a very soft light, presently. It is very meditative, in that sense. I am outdoors, yes. Soft warm air and there is very little light. There are the soft sounds of a very slim stream flowing beside me. There are above in the night sky overhead, a variety of shapes.

Some are like stars, some are like a moon you would see in your world, some are like a very distant Sun, but too close to be like a star. And there are some bands of colorations, a little bit like a rainbow up in the sky as well that are quite colorful and seemingly stationary. Not moving about at all in our perception. Very much like a rainbow up in space.

Jefferson: Wow!

Arvantis: And then I am relaxing, just being present, yes!

Jefferson: Whenever we speak of this, you always mention that you are relaxing, or taking the day off, or you are enjoying the stream. Is it that your society is more experience oriented than spiritual growth oriented?

Arvantis: How so?

Jefferson: Well, you are mostly taking the day to enjoy nature and interact with the atmosphere and the environment of your world rather than studying, or reading, or informing yourselves.

Arvantis: We gain great knowledge by simply experiencing life, just living with the spirits that are a part of our creation, a part of our world, a part of our life here.

Jefferson: So you are very connected to your planet?

Arvantis: And we are our planet too, in a sense, our planet is us. A very deep bond, connection, yes!

Jefferson: So there is spiritual growth actually.

Arvantis: Yes!

Jefferson: Fantastic! All right Arvantis! Again, thank you very much and...God bless you!

Arvantis: Thank you, we understand the humor in the statement, and we are always grateful to be blessed by you, and ourselves, and God, however anyone chooses to define that aspect of theirself.

Much joy dear one! We look forward to our interchange with you in this way in timing you would classify as your future! Much joy present with you as you spread your wings, as you lift your arms high and wide beside you. Let there be light in the delight that you are. Good day!

Jefferson: Good day! Thank you! Awesome!

Chapter 8

Living Harmoniously in Your True Design

"The more you follow your heart the best you can, the more it comes for you the ability to experience that you are living your greatest abundant joy in each moment!"

- Arvantis

February 16th, 2010

Arvantis: Wonderful to be here in this time with you! How are you this day of your time?

Jefferson: Excited to speak to you again!

Arvantis: Thank you! Always in this moment with you a joy as well! Very uplifting experiencings of interaction with you in this moment, in this avenue of sharing in light spaciousness. So we have the opportunity once again to bring forth that which you find as information to expand your understanding of who you are, of who we are, what this infinite Universe is like, and how you can tap into it, so to speak, and feel more of its joy, feel more of your infinite joyful nature!

Jefferson: Awesome! Whenever we talk…when I ask something…it seems you already know what I am going to ask. Is that what

happens?

Arvantis: I can but not all the time, no.

Jefferson: Okay. Before we go more in depth on what I would like to talk about today, I would like you to tell us what have you done since we spoke last week?

Arvantis: Nothing! Nothing at all! Not a single thing has occurred since the time we last spoke. For we've been speaking the entire time. There has been no break, no week, no passage of time for us at all. And you? You speak of a week, a passage of time, how have you filled that week?

Jefferson: Seven days have passed.

Arvantis: Very well, if you say so. How has that been for you in your experiencing of that time passage?

Jefferson: Taking one day at a time. Following the highest excitement in self- honesty, self-forgiveness, and seeing all one can get with a few daily disciplines practiced every day!

Arvantis: Very good!

Jefferson: What have you done this past week?

Arvantis: I have allowed the time to seem like there was no time at all passing by, as though I spoke to you just a moment ago in what you referred to as a week ago. So it's as though I have been sitting here the whole time. And you have gone off and created the idea of a week having passed before your life, of activities, and functions, and interactions with others in that seven days that you speak of having passed in your experiencing, in the way you created that experience. And again, I have simply been here having conversation with you as though there was but a few moments of silence that one could have a deep breath or two in between what you call a weeks ago transmission and this interaction at this moment with you now.

Jefferson: That is fascinating! In this time that I call a week, have

the both of us had opportunities to interact in other ways?

Arvantis: There are always opportunities for interactions in other ways, yes.

Jefferson: Have we?

Arvantis: Yes, well in other ways certainly, but perhaps not in ways you are familiar with.

Jefferson: What can you share about it?

Arvantis: That we are always interacting in some way, shape, and form at all moments, in all times as you create that idea of time to exist. The moments, the ways we interact that you will become aware of, have to do with what you choose to focus on or tune in to.

Jefferson: Oh.

Arvantis: You aren't missing out on anything. If you haven't experienced it, if you aren't aware of it, then there is nothing that transpired that you would have missed out on.

Jefferson: I know that I have sent to your world and my beloved brothers, the Arkoreuns, golden feathers of appreciation. Did you receive any?

Arvantis: We have sensations that come through, yes. Thank You!

Jefferson: Yes! So Arvantis, I have heard you speak a lot about the idea that synchronicity flows out of following our highest excitement and connects us to the abundance we all deserve today and all have equal access to! Could you elaborate on that?

Arvantis: Elaborate on the idea of having abundance in every moment?

Jefferson: Yes, abundance that we can experience by following our highest excitement and allowing related synchronicities to occur for us.

Arvantis: The highest excitement is yourself being of greatest abundance in the current incarnation that you are aware of being in. Only when you follow that excitement to the best of your ability do you then allow yourself to remain on that path in that experience that is of greatest abundance for you from one moment of joyfulness to the next. And there will then be in those moments nothing you feel you are missing, nothing you feel that you need. You will in each moment feel fully satisfied and fully receiving of all that you think is necessary for you to live in that particular moment, the most uplifting experience of your life.

Follow your heart as best you can in each moment and you will be able to recognize more and more so that you have all that you need to be experiencing the experiences you were choosing to create for yourself. In that sense, you will always have all that you need to be in alignment with your heart, experiencing your ecstasy, your infinite nature, in ways that are joyful for you, in ways that allow you to know you have all that you need, in ways that you feel satisfied and content, relishing each moment, excited about each moment. You have that available for you in each moment. The more you follow your heart the best you can, the more it comes for you the ability to experience that you are living your greatest abundant joy in each moment.

The more you stop looking for things and wanting things and accept that you are in each moment creating what is of greatest abundance for you, the more you will be in content, in peace with whatever it is you are experiencing, whatever it is you are creating yourself to be experiencing. And you will not feel there is something you must attain, or acquire, or achieve. You will not feel as though there is something missing, as though you must find a missing link or uncover a hidden treasure. You will simply feel fully in your ecstasy, content, abundant, wise, fully in service and in alignment with that which is of greatest purpose and meaning for you as you define those ideas and understand them.

Jefferson: Great, Thanks! I will come back to that! Now...I would like to visit more about the life of Giordano Bruno. He seemed to understand sacred geometry. How did he learn about it?

Arvantis: This is an idea that has been on your world for many generations, many centuries, quite a few eons. So then it is available for people who have an interest to connect with it and to then learn and to share their understanding of it in whatever way they choose.

Jefferson: How did he play with this idea?

Arvantis: Well, there was the idea that all things were connected, in a sense, some geometry of sacred teachings can activate within a person the remembering that all things are connected and so, you could say, that the geometrical drawings and teachings are like a permission slip, if you will, to allow yourself to remember this connection with all things.

Jefferson: Okay.

Arvantis: It is, in a sense, a key that can open the door and allow oneself to step into a room and when they are there in that room they remember they are connected to all things. It is one of the ways that you have put into your society to recall, to reconnect, to remember more how it is you are connected to all things, a part of all things. It is like a tool to reconnect, to activate the memory that you are connected to all things. It is but one tool, one way to play in that way!

Jefferson: Yes. And has he asked you something in that regards as far as knowledge goes that relates to sacred geometry?

Arvantis: There were some questions at times to help understand things that came as a result of the sacred geometry. Not anything we are aware of as far as questions about geometry itself for there were those there that were able to provide information sufficient enough to make that individual you speak of to then have the activations take place so this individual had more of a remembrance, an activation, a reconnection, of the sense of being one with all things. And so the questions were then about the idea of being connected to all things, as a result of having studied some ideas around sacred geometry.

Jefferson: Isn't there a fear of some sort within the human being that when he gets connected to all things he may lose his individuality?

Arvantis: There is not fear in the human being, but there are humans who create an idea of being frightened of such a thing. Fear is simply a misperception of something that a person creates and tunes in to, but it isn't something that's actually in them, like their organs are in them.

Jefferson: So when I know with every fiber of my being that we are one with the all, that knowing will raise my vibration?

Arvantis: There is great upliftment in frequency, yes!

Jefferson: Do I have to stop existing in one place and start living in another?

Arvantis: It occurs automatically but not necessarily in terms of living on a different physical planet.

Jefferson: Oh. Is it to get in touch with different versions of people?

Arvantis: And different frequencies of experiencing of the infinite Universe.

Jefferson: But when you interact with people, if you are in that high-speed vibration frequency, then you have to go back to the mundane way of dealing with things. So you have to kind of go back and forth?

Arvantis: You can at first live in that idea of bridging between those two ideas, yes, but you can live in the physical world and not go back into what you referred to as mundane world, mundane ways.

Jefferson: Okay.

Arvantis: So there can be a growth learning process. Getting fully across the bridge and realizing you no longer need that bridge.

Jefferson: And how can a person do that?

Arvantis: Through their desire, their following of their heart, listening, learning, growing, cherishing, and appreciating each moment as best as they can. The guidance then will come from within for which steps will be most supportive to gaining that ability and then attaining that spaciousness of existence and awareness.

Jefferson: Wow. So Arvantis, from 1592 to 1600, Giordano Bruno stayed in a prison. I mean, eight years behind the bars. So, it is to assume that in those years, that particular being that I was, would have done many things so he would not get bored. What can you tell me about the life of Giordano Bruno during those eight years?

Arvantis: We have the idea there was opportunity to deal with the concepts of separation and having the ability to connect to life that could bring joy without needing the physical perception of freedom. The person could experience great joy while seemingly in the physical world being limited in a cell, in a prison cell. The idea then became clearer that what one is experiencing isn't always then based on whether or not they can move about in their physical world freely or not. The physical world provides opportunity for a person to explore their consciousness, their inner realm, to create the idea of freedom or to create the idea of prison, of limitation, and separation. But being thus then limited in a cell, in a prison cell, there was the opportunity to realize that what is occurring in the physical world really isn't the ultimate decider as to how a person experiences their life, for there can be great joy in the sense of freedom and flexibility in one's experience of life without having physical freedom or the physical flexibility to move about from one location to the other at will, without being locked into a cellular building.

The idea then was learning that how one experiences the sense of freedom in life is entirely up to their own conscious creation and not a factor of what is going on in the external world and whether or not they have particular freedoms in the physical world. Freedom comes from within whether you are walking about the world freely or in a prison cell.

Jefferson: So basically the idea is not to let our environment build the feelings within us but rather have the feelings within build the environment around us?

Arvantis: You could say that he came to realize more that what is occurring in his experiencing is based on what he chooses to focus on and create and not on what is happening in the external, physical world.

Jefferson: Wow!

Arvantis: That idea then to live within, rather than going outward. Not to determine who you are based on what is happening in the outer physical world. He learned to step away from looking outside to figure out who he was and what he could do or not do. He realized that what was important then was to be within to determine what is real for him and what he is or is not. Thus then, this gave him enormous freedom for what was taking place in the physical world around him, for there is in the physical world a perception that many things are out of your control, or influence. So when he realized they aren't determining what he can or cannot feel and experience, he gave himself great freedom from that outer world that previously had seemed to be beyond his control.

Jefferson: At what age, if at all, did Giordano Bruno discover that he had a past life around the teacher that many refer to today as Jesus, a teacher that I then also had a lifetime around?

Arvantis: That was the age that was most in alignment with his ability to appreciate that understanding and to work with it most beneficially.

Jefferson: And around what age was that?

Arvantis: Again, as we said, when it was most appropriate for him, when he was most skilled of the wisdom to understand how to work with that connection.

Jefferson: How did he discover he had a past life around Jesus, and once he did discover it, how did it impact his behavior?

Arvantis: It allowed him to feel more content with his choice to create his life based on what was occurring within him, to create from within his life experience, to feel more trusting of that process and to let go more and more so of looking outside into the physical world for indications of who he was. He recognized more readily that the external world was not the place to go to determine who he was. To ask the outside world to tell him who he was is something he let go of. To look for the external world to give him accolades and applause, was something he learned to let go of. To look to the outside world to be given honors, was something he learned to let go of. And then more easily and with greater force of focus, he then honored himself. He gave thanks to himself for himself.

He appreciated himself more and more and thus then that was something he began to understand from that lifetime of his that was coexisting with the being you referred to as Yeshua, or Jesus, or Joshua, whichever name you prefer.

Jefferson: So in that past life of Giordano's, which was also a past life of mine, how was the encounter when I met Jesus for the first time?

Arvantis: It was something that was unusual, uplifting, somewhat re-patterning, illuminating, discombobulating, a little bit disorienting. And thus there was a moment of having to sit down then to catch one's breath, so to speak, to allow for frequency adjustments to occur so this being you were in that lifetime could come back into a more aware and focused state in that moment of experiencing contact with this being of Yeshua.

Yeshua had a way of, in a sense, overwhelming people at times, and you could say it was occurring to that person, to this you of that lifetime.

Jefferson: Once this being caught his breath, what happened?

Arvantis: There was simply a moment of several minutes of silence. Allowing for a new sensation to move through the body in terms of this persons sensing of feelings in the body, warm undulations, waves of energy, soothing, warm flowing, feeling like fluid of warm liquids flowing through the physiology, feeling very much like an internal massage of warm fluids flowing through the physiology and feeling very at ease, happy, content, in a state of bliss, you could say, ecstasy, you could call it. It had a depth that was quite new for this being in that moment in their lifetime. This went on for about ten minutes with silence.

Jefferson: Okay!

Arvantis: At which time then the being, Yeshua, had in a rather acknowledging way, moved on for that day. As if to say, goodbye for now, until we meet again.

Jefferson: I see, so that was the first time. And, I know that you can time travel, so was that at night, day, morning?

Arvantis: This occurred in the evening hours around sunset.

Jefferson: And in what city?

Arvantis: This was in the southern region of Eastern Europe. The name for that area isn't the same now. It is today in a region of Hungary, but then it was of a different term.

Jefferson: So that first encounter with Jesus, it got me thinking...I would assume I wouldn't have been able to sleep that night? How did I digest the encounter?

Arvantis: In the way we have spoken of, and then there was quickly after that a movement into sleep.

Jefferson: Oh...I see. Okay. And when was the next time that he met this master teacher?

Arvantis: There was an outdoor gathering some weeks later.

Jefferson: Okay.

Arvantis: You had the opportunity to interact briefly, with words on an individual basis, and also to listen to this person sharing information with those who were at the gathering.

Jefferson: Fantastic! And can you share what the conversation was about?

Arvantis: There was acknowledgement of the "activation" that caused the flowing of the warm energies and the sense of greater peace, the sense of being more at one with All That Is. However, *activation* was not the word that was used. This person shared his experience of that activation with Yeshua. Thanking that being of Yeshua, but not asking him how it was that Yeshua was able to bring about such an experience. The activation had occurred in a fashion that was beyond ability to comprehend, and thus then, this person was not in a state of mind to ask questions of how it was done. So the conversation was a sharing of words to provide thanks, acknowledgement, to express gratitude.

Jefferson: And then Yeshua said great, or good job, or…?

Arvantis: Very little was spoken by Yeshua, for there was an understanding with this being Yeshua of what was occurring and he realized that words were of little function, unnecessary for that being – you, in that timing. That was understood as well by the being you were in that lifetime, and so not looking for a long dialogue or any specific spoken message to come from Yeshua, simply there to express gratitude. That was a great completion, in that moment of interaction, that being that was you in that moment with Yeshua, a great sense of being fulfilled, having had that brief individual conversation.

Jefferson: I understand he became a follower of Yeshua.

Arvantis: There were teachings, sharings, understandings that he was in great strength of resonance with. And you could say then there was that way of following, of choosing to behave and learn and live in alignment with the teachings that Yeshua had shared. You could say that, in a sense, was a following.

Jefferson: So I understand as well that in that particular lifetime I met Shaun, the channeler.

Arvantis: Yes.

Jefferson: And at what point did that happen?

Arvantis: At an early age.

Jefferson: Oh. So we played together?

Arvantis: There were those opportunities.

Jefferson: And how did we meet?

Arvantis: You had families that were coexisting in that community. Parents with similar ideas. Neighbors in the same community.

Jefferson: I understand he was part of the Essene.

Arvantis: There was some familiar interaction with the Essene. Not born into the Essene.

Jefferson: You're referring to the being that I was or he was?

Arvantis: He was born of a different understanding and came into learn of the Essene way and was fascinated with it and thus then he took action to become a part of that community for a period of some years before then moving out into other ideologies, and other communities, and other groups of other form and fashion in teachings and sharings.

Jefferson: You mean him?

Arvantis: Yes, the channel.

Jefferson: What about me?

Arvantis: You had some contact with the Essene, but we don't sense that you were born as an Essene in that community in that lifetime.

Jefferson: I see.

Arvantis: You were somewhat more removed from the Essene group and gatherings at that timing, primarily due to your own interests but also due to the influence your parents had on you in that time.

Jefferson: Was I one of Yeshua's apostles?

Arvantis: Not directly one of those apostles that are spoken of in your religious books. The names of some of those are accurate, but some of them are not. He had several individuals that could be called apostles, and many of them are not identified in any book on your planet at this timing. The names are not in any written form on your planet at this time.

There was a large group that could be called apostles and then there was the James, who was what could be called an apostle, yes. But not then necessarily the one that is sometimes spoken of in biblical passages. Some of those are, for various reasons, are inaccurate. Some of them are manufactured. Some of them lost in translations or mistranslated.

Jefferson: Oh, I see. Okay. Enough on that for now. The idea about following our highest excitement. I would like to visit that a bit more with you.

Arvantis: Yes!

Jefferson: Isn't it irresponsible to tell people, "everything is going to be all right if you just follow your highest excitement," unless you also teach them the four Laws of Creation?

Arvantis: Are you suggesting people need to understand the Laws of Creation before they would be able to follow their joy?

Jefferson: Well, if someone doesn't understand the Laws of Creation and I suggest they follow their heart...well...then I see a blank stare on their face or they might laugh and the first question that they usually ask is, "how am I going to support myself if I just follow my highest excitement?" It's as though they think what gives them pleasure can't also bring them abundance in a financial way. Can you expand and comment on that?

Arvantis: Your society has taught for thousands of years the idea that you have to work hard, you have to plan ahead, you have to organize, you have to orchestrate, you have to put your nose to the grindstone, so to speak, in order to be successful in your world. This teaching is something you do that keeps your society disconnected from the true guidance mechanism that is built-in to your biology. It's in your DNA. Your internal guidance mechanism exists within All That Is, and it guides you to simply follow your heart, the sensation that feels good!

The way your society has been teaching itself removes you from this true internal and heartfelt guidance mechanism. As a society, you have found ways that disconnect yourselves from your true internal guidance mechanism so you could explore great depths of limitation, and separation, and struggle, and sacrifice, and compromise, and having to work hard. That is a choice you wanted to explore, an experience you wanted to play with upon your Earthian stage, the theater of humans on Earth. And so there are a magnificent and vast number of ways and belief systems that have been engrained in your belief systems and become embedded in your DNA like little software programs that are constantly feeding you information, telling you subconsciously what you must do to survive on Earth. These unnatural programs taught into your DNA, in a sense, send you data that is the opposite of your actual nature and what you should truly be doing if you want to be in a feeling of your actual abundance and be following your heart, in that sense. With the, in a sense, corrupted DNA, when such a person hears all they need to do is to simply follow their heart, well that goes against everything within their corrupted genetics and the generational teachings from thousands of years of education and upbringing within your society. So there is then this response that such a suggestion is silly, without merit, without credibility, without potential to truly serve such a function.

Jefferson: Okay.

Arvantis: And thus then, because "what you put out is what you get back," third Law of Creation, when they don't believe it will work and they put that thought out into the world, they will then get back experiences that will confirm for them that it doesn't work. But of course it is working, they are getting back what they are putting out. It's just that what they're putting out is coming from the thousands of years of discordant teachings about the nature of their true self and their heart's powerful guidance capability.

When someone doesn't understand the idea and also negates the idea that following their heart will bring them complete abundance, then they are working against their actual nature. They will be functioning at odds with themselves, creating friction, and then it will feel as though they do have to work hard to get through each day. They will have to create other ways to survive. They will use their ego mind, their physical mind, to create plans and procedures, and strategies, and processes that they think then will provide for them a successful life. This is hard work for many people. It doesn't feel good for many who do that. It feels as though they are missing something important in life when they live that way. All of the hard work and the sense of missing meaningful things in life is their internal guidance mechanism letting them know, hey, you aren't doing it in alignment with yourself. You weren't designed to do it that way. That's why it is hard work. You can let go of that and start following your heart and moving into the effortless flow of your true design. Believe that following your heart will support you and you will be supported one hundred percent, we guarantee you! It will work! It always has. It always will. It cannot not work. It flows with the nature of Existence. Follow your heart and you will always be provided for. Trust that mechanism and you will discover over time, step by step, one realization after another realization, one light bulb going off after another light bulb going off in terms of your "ah-hah I get it" moments, you will discover that it becomes easier for you to accept the simplicity of how you can create abundance and joy in your life moment by moment, day to day, without any interruption at all!

There is an enormous and powerfully disruptive consciousness pattern, a discordant consciousness belief system within the collective consciousness that, in a sense, is designed to laugh at the idea that following your heart is all you have to do. So then, do not be surprised when people look at you with a blank stare on their face or laugh at you. They are simply swimming in the currents of their collective conscious belief systems and unknowingly going against the flow of the nature of Existence itself. They are choosing to swim upstream, as an analogy, just as salmons do in your rivers of your Northwest America. They are swimming upstream so they can then have the opportunity to multiply with others of like mind and then create more of like mind. Before the newborns are birthed into the currents of life, they flow downstream and go easily with the flow of the nature of Existence. But upon their birth, they will then find currents that are like thoughts that go against their actual nature and cause them to swim upstream. They will fight the current as the genetics placed into them by their ancestors teachings taught them to do so they can once again spawn upstream with more like minded individuals and create even more people who, in a sense, go against the flow of Creation. It is a pattern that is strong that has existed in your world for many thousands of years and so it feels comfortable fighting the flow of following your heart's joy.

Jefferson: How can those who are interested to live within and as their highest excitement achieve this?

Arvantis: We suggest you follow your heart as best you can. You are free to create as many other disruptive or discordant ideas as you want. You have eternity. You have your lifetime in this lifetime and in other lifetimes that you can incarnate in where you can create similar discordant ideas. There is no limit on the length of time you can create discordant belief systems that are going against your actual effortless, beautifully imaginative, and creative ability. You can go at odds with yourself for as long as you like in any numbers of ways you choose, or you can simply follow your heart to the best of your ability in each moment. If others want to laugh about that, they can. If you want to hang out with their choice to laugh at you, then you can experience more people who laugh at that idea. If you want to be with people who are more in resonance with your idea of following your heart, you thus then will attract more people of that idea. You will then be able to flow together, and swim downstream, and live a life of greater joy that will be full of all the abundance in the ways that you know are providing the most meaningful and purposeful life you could ever ask for in that incarnation. And you will have great gratitude moment by moment for the effortless joy of life you are experiencing through your own creative choices.

Jefferson: It seems that I can share this idea of "following your heart" with another human being who then might respond by laughing at me. And I suppose it's best to simply allow them to be who they are and have unconditional love for them. But some other people might tell me I should instead respond by saying, "no, no, no" when someone laughs at me.

Arvantis: You can accept that belief if you want, it's up to you!

Jefferson: Oh, no, I understand that belief to be "flawed" but what would you suggest is going on with people who think like that —

Arvantis: Well, it's simply a belief. All beliefs are equal. You can say they are all flawed, or none are flawed, or some are flawed. But in terms of their actual nature of existence, they simply are. They are all neutral. You can say one is good, or bad, or flawed, or perfect. It is simply how you are choosing to define it. The Universe accepts and considers all beliefs to be of equal value.

Jefferson: Okay!

Arvantis: Some are opposite the actual nature of existence and some are in alignment with the actual nature of existence. The beliefs that are in alignment with the actual nature of existence will provide the person that has that belief a greater sense of joy. People who have beliefs that are at odds with the actual nature of existence will then experience a greater sense of tension, and disease, and conflict in their life. Which do you prefer? It's up to you! The choice is always for you to make!

Jefferson: Okay. Very well. To change topic Arvantis, the descriptions that you share of your world's environment can take people on meditative journeys. So would you be so kind as to give us a bit of your surroundings?

Arvantis: I am presently in a space of being outdoors. Living in a space under the stars. There is the sense of comfort of the infinite present, of being sustained by the planet that I am presently on, of being supported by all that I am and all that this physical world before me that I also am is presenting itself an opportunity to see, to live, to share within. I am feeling very infinite and joyful. Feeling very at ease with the environment that is around me, the life forms that are present. I am having a breath move through my body, out of my body, back in, back out, and feeling very at ease in this environment in which I am in presently. I am enjoying the rich depth of life's support for me, appreciation of me, gratitude for me, and I too am in mutual appreciation of all that I am presently aware of and experiencing.

In a sense, I am breathing it in, even as I breathe in the air before me. Bringing it into my being, sharing the joy of my physiology with All That Is in this environment before me. The stars. The landscape. All here in support of one another mutually. Interacting joyously with one another. Providing nourishment, healing, so at home in a depth of peacefulness, so content, so assured of the purpose for me now, as always for me feeling that I am in alignment with that. And the meaning for me of All That Is, is rich, and apparent, and fulfilling and being fulfilled in each breath that I am taking and that is moving out of my body with each exhalation.

That is just a taste, a touch of my present environment from which I channel through for you today on this line of communication that the channel sometimes refers to as a "we phone." As though he were a speakerphone in which I was speaking through and you and all others who listen-in can then hear the conversation too. We can communicate in this way through this speakerphone in which the channel is symbolically a "we phone" that allows our societies to interact and communicate in this way. There is great joy here in this moment of sharing with you and with the "we phone," the channel. Thank you!

Jefferson: Can you briefly describe the colors that you see around you there?

Arvantis: The colors are in this time, as I understand your question, the colors in all that I have described are very rich. Therein you can learn if you listen again or read again the description, you can learn to see those colors in the descriptions and the statements I have just made. You can learn to feel those colors for they exist in a different form than you are so used to seeing colors as being with your eyes as reds, or blues, or greens, or yellows, or oranges. You can see these colors if you meditate on the description that I have just shared with you.

We ask then to let that be the way to experience the colors that are present with me here in this timing and also with those others who are here too. For there are several Arkoreuns present who are listening in. And there are those from the Yahyel present. There are those from the Sassani present. There are other societies of what you would consider extraterrestrials, some are human, and some are of other life forms. All are very wise, very intelligent, very uplifting, very supportive for the process of learning to be in your heart and allowing for the nature of Creation to become more aware for you so that you can live with greater abundance in the ways that are of great meaning and feel of full purpose for you all as a society and as individuals as well.

Jefferson: Wow…did you just say that the Yahyel and the Sassani are there? Like physically present?

Arvantis: There are those from those societies present, yes!

Jefferson: Well, tell them I send them my highest love and light!

Arvantis: They hear, thank you, yes! Much joy and love for your sharing for them!

Jefferson: Can anybody from any other planet that comes to your planet have a love relationship with a race that is different than theirs?

Arvantis: Yes.

Jefferson: That can occur?

Arvantis: Yes.

Jefferson: But they cannot reproduce because they are from a different race?

Arvantis: There are some instances where it can still occur.

Jefferson: Very well, so Arvantis, any parting thoughts?

Arvantis: That will do for now! We thank you for the rich sharing and the questions. Some were quite personal for you and we understand it takes great courage to be willing to do that, knowing there will be information thus then in a book format, at least in book format, that will be presented to others in a public way. Great joy in your choice we receive from having that courage to share those personal ideas and experiences of yourself. Thank you for being willing to move in that light, to be bold in that fashion, for there will be many who will have and intake joy in having read those excerpts, those personal transmissions, sharings from you!

Jefferson: I thank you very much for your heart of appreciation, your heart of passion, and your heart of compassion for

understanding where we are in our growth. With everything that we do, you seem to have an understanding, and a caring, and an appreciation, and a knowing that all is well and fine! So thank you very much Arvantis for everything!

Arvantis: Lovely, thank you! It's all right. It's all here. It's all beautiful, all the time, 24/7, seven days a week, twenty-four hours every day. It's all right. It's all here, and it's beautiful and it's present for you to tap into in an infinite number of ways that cannot get away from you if you choose to follow your heart more fully, to embrace that beautiful design that exists within all life. If you choose to, over time you will more clearly be able to live beyond *all right*. You will be in the joy, the ecstasy, beautifully so! Without any interruption at all. Without any opposition at all. Without any delusion at all. And you will be a fantasy realized, in a sense, you will feel your innocence, your infinite beauty, your wisdom. An abundance of joy will be yours without end.

Thank you dear one once again for having taken the time to be a part of this interaction. To put together these questions and to share these insights so that together we may create a third new reality that then in the sharing of this information that has come forth, bring about a closer frequency with your world, with our world. Galactic family, genetic children, genetic family that is a family unlike any anyone on your world has come to experience yet. It is a family that brings tears of joy, a family that supports you in joyous ways without question. It is always there to provide that support without a moments hesitation, and it is always supporting you wonderfully so. It is a family that will, for your society, completely redefine what a family can be.

We assure you these transactions, these transmissions, can help facilitate that day when our world and yours can thus then come together in physiology and share face to face, eye to eye, hand to hand, heart to heart, together. And in that timing share vast amounts of understanding. The likes of which you haven't even begun to explore with your imaginations.

So dear one, thank you! Good day and much love from all who are present here to all who are present there with you. Much love! Good day!

Jefferson: Good day. Thank you!

Chapter 9

The Prime Creator Is All of Us

"Existence itself is actually meaningless. It lets you give it meaning. And by understanding that, there is a very expansive, meaningful, and fulfilling purpose that you will be able to more fully experience."

- Arvantis

March 23rd, 2010

Arvantis: Very well, how are you doing this day of your time, in this moment, how are you?

Jefferson: What a pleasure!

Arvantis: Delightful to be in this interaction in this way with you again!

Jefferson: It does feel like the first time!

Arvantis: Very well! Thank you for that refreshing experiential sharing.

Jefferson: How have you been?

Arvantis: Wonderful! I have been exploring, examining, and creating together in new worlds today, in this moment with you as well. We explore the opportunities to expand our understandings together to bring forth information from our perspective that may in that way then help your understanding and those in your society who may come upon the information in whatever forms you choose to share it.

Jefferson: All right! When I release a resistance of some sort, in the sense of shattering a belief paradigm that was keeping me from having 20-20 vision of spiritual awareness, does every aspect of me in every time and space reality feel it to some extent?

Arvantis: Do you feel it to some extent?

Jefferson: Yes, well...I know I am existing at the same time in many time-space realities, so does my releasing of resistance have a positive affect on those aspects of me?

Arvantis: Yes, it does!

Jefferson: Okay. Since we are the same soul, is everything that I have learned so far and will learn in this lifetime, is it also within you...sort of like...treasures of wisdom that are collected from my experiences on this planet?

Arvantis: You could say that.

Jefferson: Are all timelines happening at the same time?

Arvantis: Yes. The timeline of past, present, and future is an experience you are creating.

Jefferson: Okay.

Arvantis: It isn't real. It is an illusion, but it is an experience that provides you with opportunities that you find enjoyable. There isn't anything wrong with that idea of creating the illusion of past, present, and future.

Jefferson: Okay.

Arvantis: It's simply a choice you are excited about, and it's a choice that your collective chooses to make quite frequently in your world today.

Jefferson: But Arvantis, doesn't it work like this, I am living here and once I finish this lifetime I will make my lovely transition and then in 357 years in the future I will be born as Arvantis?

Arvantis: That is one timeline. It may not apply to all that you have available to explore in terms of other opportunities of timelines.

Jefferson: Would you say that is to complicated for a human being to understand?

Arvantis: To some degree, but the idea in the way you presented it, it makes it sound like you perceive that there is only one train headed to one station, one destination. There are several trains leading in many different directions, several destinations. Many possible life timelines.

Jefferson: Okay.

Arvantis: So perhaps loosen up a bit about how you perceive that idea of where you might go after you transition, what directions and destinations you may choose to tune in to after you transition. For there are more than the one you have spoken of.

Jefferson: I think I understand. Since we are living simultaneous lifetimes, the fact that my train goes towards one direction does not cancel all the other directions that the train could have gone and probably has, but I am just not focused on the other ones now.

Arvantis: It's not that the train *could have gone.* It is going. And yes, because you don't focus on the other ones you don't experience those train rides.

Jefferson: So the others exist and are as real as the ride that I was aware of?

Arvantis: Yes.

Jefferson: It is just that I am not focused there?

Arvantis: Correct. In our experience, that would be a more appropriate way to gather, and explore, and experience, and to think about that idea.

Jefferson: But right now, I am Jefferson, I am Arvantis, I am the Zeta guy, and I am the Andromeda guy. So in my perception and comprehension of this idea, we are all the same soul, but existing in different timeframes?

Arvantis: You all exist as the same one infinite being that is creating the idea that you have other timelines or other lifetimes. But these are things that you are all creating, illusions. For you all actually only exist here and now, in that sense.

Even here and now is something that isn't really existing. You just create that idea of here and now, and we speak of it in a way that you can have more of an ability to focus into the infinite existence that is your actual nature, that is timeless, that isn't even actually a moment. It simply is.

Jefferson: I see.

Arvantis: So that then could be something that is perhaps beyond the scope of your awareness to really grasp in your present physical state of consciousness, and that is perfectly appropriate for the choices that you are exploring in your present life as a collective and as an individual.

Jefferson: So in order to experience life, I separated from All That Is, and created an individualized part of that All That Is which is me?

Arvantis: The separation is simply a creation through your imagination. It is an illusion. You haven't really separated from the One that is the All, All That Is.

Jefferson: Okay. The philosopher called Socrates said, "the unexamined life is not worth living." Other philosophers have said, "Know thyself." As I read your teachings and the ideas you share, I

realize that you guide people inwards in a way they can get to know more of themselves. Is that a bit of what you are sharing here?

Arvantis: There can be that sense, "guiding inwards" so someone can more fully realize the infinite expansiveness of their beingness.

Jefferson: And Descartes said, "I think therefore I am." From that idea, would you find appropriate to conclude that everything we see is meaningless?

Arvantis: Because he is, he can think! So you might look at it the other way as well.

Jefferson: Would you say that again?

Arvantis: Because he is, he can think.

Jefferson: Oh.

Arvantis: If he did not exist, he could not think.

Jefferson: Okay.

Arvantis: That's just another way to look at the idea. It comes down a bit to semantics too, and perhaps how he was defining the term "I am" and "I think" when he made that statement. We are just suggesting you could look at it the other way as well. He is and therefore he can think.

Jefferson: I just remembered another quote that is from Winston Churchill, "You create your own universe as you go along." Does that mean I have given everything I see all the meaning that it has for me?

Arvantis: Whatever meaning you experience in life is a result of the meaning you have placed into that experience, how you have chosen to define the experience. You only get back meaning as a result of the meaning you put out, the definitions and beliefs that you put out.

Jefferson: Is that related to the third Law of Creation?

Arvantis: Yes! "What you put out is what you get back!"

Jefferson: And if you track it back a little bit, it seems I can't put out something if I don't already have it within my heart?

Arvantis: You have an infinite potential of what you can put out, for you're an infinite oneness of beingness.

Jefferson: All right.

Arvantis: Therefore you can then get back an infinite number of experiences.

Jefferson: I have the humble attitude to say that I probably don't know and don't understand everything. Of all the stuff that I interact with in my life, lots of details might simply pass unnoticed to me given my inability to fully perceive All That Is. So that attitude can be an important factor in having some sort of direction in life, would you not say that?

Arvantis: You can.

Jefferson: In your world, do you guys just follow your heart, and whatever comes is good and...you know, just having fun and enjoying life?

Arvantis: Yes! Is that too hard to accept? Does it sound boring?

Jefferson: No! No, no!

Arvantis: Unchallenging?

Jefferson: Not at all! There was a professor, an American educator, that said, "Wisdom is meaningless until your own experience has given it meaning." So would you say that the thoughts we think are also meaningless?

Arvantis: Existence has no meaning fundamentally. So how you experience existence and the meaning for you of anything is determined by how you choose to define your existence and what meaning you choose to give various experiences in your life. Existence itself is actually meaningless. It lets you give it meaning. And by understanding that, there is a very expansive, meaningful, and fulfilling purpose that you will be able to more fully experience.

Jefferson: In your world, how do you define the idea of the prime Creator?

Arvantis: I am that which is the Source, the Source is that which is you, that is all things, all life. And in that existence, that infinite Source, I am choosing to have this particular focus of that infinite Source that I could call my lifetime in this present incarnation in ways that I find most enjoyable, and most opportune, and most representative of the frequency of the one infinite Source of myself that I choose to explore, that I choose to flow within, that I choose to be an expresser of as an artistic craftsman of life expression, as a sculptor of a life experience of the infinite one that I am, that you are, the prime Creator that I am, that you are, that we all are. I choose to experience the infinite, one Creator that we are in this way, in this fashion for it excites me the most to be doing so, to be focusing in this moment of my creationship.

Jefferson: I see.

Arvantis: I am the prime Creator, you are, we all are, and we exist in all levels. All gradients, all frequencies, all extensions. Even if those specific beings on all the different levels and frequencies and extensions aren't aware that they are the prime Creator. That doesn't exclude the reality that they are, for it would be impossible for them not to be.

Jefferson: Okay.

Arvantis: To create the illusion that they are not the prime Creator, yes, that you can create in an infinite number of ways, just as you can create many, many movies, or plays, or television shows, or novels, or science fiction books. You can create many different ideas and experiences. But no matter how removed through extensions, or levels, or lack of knowledge they may seem to be, the prime Creator they all are, for "the one is the all, and the all are the one."

Jefferson: Good, great. Fantastic! So Arvantis, what is the meaning of life, in that sense?

Arvantis: Your choice! What would you like it to mean for you! Existence does not have a built in meaning.

Jefferson: Okay.

Arvantis: You have the ability with, "what you put out is what you get back" — the third Law of Creation — to create your own idea of what life's meaning is for you. And because of the fourth law, "change is the only constant except the first three laws," you can change what you are putting out. You can change what the meaning of life is for you and thus get back a different experience of what life's meaning is for you. It's your choice!

Jefferson: Okay!

Arvantis: Creator's choice! You are the Creator. What is your choice? Allow then, we suggest, for it to come more fully from your heart. To feel exciting and uplifting and fill you with exuberance and radiance of joyful laughter and a sense of, for you, purpose in that meaningful life. Our suggestion only.

Jefferson: When you say, "What you put out is what you get back," the quality of things that I put out is based on my level of consciousness and awareness of my creatorship?

Arvantis: Yes, you cannot experience something you are not the vibration of!

Jefferson: Oh.

Arvantis: But you can change your vibration and experience new things. What you might define and label as more expansive, more evolved, you can do that.

Jefferson: I haven't heard you speak much about vibrations. Is vibration the thoughts we think, the emotions we have, and the motivation we have to take action in the physical world? Is it the

amalgamation of all of those ideas that become a signal or "vibration" that we give off that then attracts to us experiences that are in resonance with this vibration?

Arvantis: Yes.

Jefferson: You also spoke about four Universal Laws of Creation. Could you share with me what these laws are and how they work in your world?

Arvantis: There is the idea of how the Universe — how Isness, All That Is, the Infinite, All Life, whatever you want to call it — how it functions. "You exist," is the first Law of Creation.

Jefferson: Okay.

Arvantis: Second law, "The one is the all, and the all are the one."

Jefferson: Okay.

Arvantis: Third law, "What you put out is what you get back."

Jefferson: Okay.

Arvantis: The fourth law, "Change is the only constant." (Everything changes except the first three laws which never change.)

Jefferson: So that "I exist" never changes?

Arvantis: Yes.

Jefferson: That "the one is the all, and the all are the one" never changes?

Arvantis: Yes.

Jefferson: And the idea that "what I put out is what I get back" never changes?

Arvantis: Yes.

Jefferson: Hmm.

Arvantis: And what you put out changes — from the fourth law, "everything changes" — so what you get back will change.

Jefferson: In what ways, if you can share, have you changed since last time we spoke?

Arvantis: Every way, all the ways, always.

Jefferson: And when you speak about vibration and the way emotion runs in our physical level, I was wondering about its relationship with the material world. There is a person called Walter Russell who said, "The farther any emotion strays away from love the more that emotion poisons the body." What do you see within the human in regards to how emotions impact our bodies?

Arvantis: There is the emotional energy body, which is a vibratory body around your more dense physical body. The emotional body is more fluid and perhaps invisible to your eyes. For some people it's invisible to their sense of feeling since they are numb. There is with this emotional body more fluidity, more flexibility, a higher vibration. It brings forth new ideas and it can hold on to old ideas. It has the ability to influence the denser physical body.

With emotions, you can create changes in your organs in ways that will allow those organs to be more fluid, to be more flowing, to be more free, to be more whole, to be more healthy in terms of the way you define the idea of health, and to feel good physiologically whenever these emotions that you choose to tune in to are more in alignment with your actual nature and your heart's guidance.

The more you tune in to your heart the more the physical body will be in resonance with the emotional body. This will allow you to feel more happy and be healthier to create your life more effectively. You will more immediately bring about results that you prefer to have manifested in your world.

There is then as an opposite to that idea, the idea that if you aren't allowing yourself to experience emotional ideas that are in alignment with your actual nature and your heart's guidance, it causes the physical body to be in a denser vibration and to close down. It causes the physical body to be more disconnected from the fluidity of the emotional body's higher understanding, higher vibratory wavelength. This then disconnects the physical body to varying degrees, which can cause the flesh to degenerate, to decline in health the way you define the idea of heath and sickness. The physical body will become more rigid which allows then for a person to become more stagnate and to have less ability to create what they prefer. They become like a stone trying to rest on the surface of water. Generally, the stone will simply sink to the bottom and be lost. Do you follow this so far?

Jefferson: Yes!

Arvantis: There is then the emotional body. If you allow it to, it has the ability to connect you with the sensorial feelings that come from the heart. Heart vibrations move very well through the emotional body. Give sensorial feelings more importance in your life by learning to feel them, to hear them, and to be comfortable with their sensations such as joy, love, happiness, pleasure. The more you connect with heart sensorial feelings and let them move through your life as a form of guidance to be doing in each moment that which feels good to you, then they will become a vibratory wave that flows through the physiology of your physical body more and more frequently.

Heart sensorial feelings will "breeze like a soft wind" through your physiology, through your organs, through your tissues, to your cellular structures, and connect to your DNA, in a way that frees up all of that body, all of that flesh, so that it can be more whole, more healthy, more vital, and more in resonance with the vortex of your heart's truer nature of vibration.

This then allows for your body to be softer, lighter — and while perhaps appearing solid like a stone — it will be capable of being in a more whole emotional and physical resonance that is connected with the heart in a way that allows the body to be like a feather, or a duck, floating on a surface of water. This allows you to thus then be able to be in the presence of the sunlight that brings forth vision to see more of the landscape before you, making it more simple to float forward and go where you prefer to be at any given moment of your life in physicality.

Jefferson: Hmm.

Arvantis: So that's one idea to consider. Do you have any ideas in that area you would like to explore further?

Jefferson: Yes. So in terms of the idea of "cause and effect," the physical is the effect from that which is non-physical, and that which is non-physical, like emotions, is the cause?

Arvantis: There is that, in a sense, but your physical can also be the cause that effects the emotional as well, the non-physical. It can go both ways.

Jefferson: There is a non-physical teacher by the name of Abraham who says that a belief is only a thought that you keep thinking. So all a person must do is keep thinking the ideal life they want to experience and they will then have their dreams manifested?

Arvantis: Yes.

Jefferson: Can you share your thoughts on that idea?

Arvantis: That is what you are doing here, yes.

Jefferson: What do you mean?

Arvantis: What you put out is what you get back.

Jefferson: Oh.

Arvantis: You are putting out thoughts with your beliefs, your definitions about life, what you believe life to be.

Jefferson: Okay.

Arvantis: Your thoughts, yes. Your emotions, yes. Your attitudes, yes. Your actions, yes. These are all components. These are all ingredients. Not just a thought isolated from emotions, isolated from actions.

Jefferson: Okay.

Arvantis: They are not, in that sense, separate. They work together.

Jefferson: Okay.

Arvantis: But for simplification, it is simple to say, "a thought that you keep thinking," keep putting out. As more people begin to get a handle on that simple idea, you can begin providing more details by adding the idea of emotions and actions, which contribute with the thoughts you keep thinking. This gives it more of the whole picture of what it is you are putting out that is thus then bringing back to you the experiences you are having each day of your life.

Jefferson: I remember Ishuwa saying in our previous book, "You are all great magicians creating a show in which you have, in a sense, pulled your heart out of the hat and made it disappear."

Arvantis: Yes!

Jefferson: So it seems that he is alluding to the idea that the heart may seem to have disappeared but the magicians that did that are still here.

Arvantis: Yes.

Jefferson: Giordano Bruno said that there is a magic that each one of us carries within that reflects the divine existence of prime Creator in all creation. So magic is everywhere!

Arvantis: You can say that. You can define magic in many different ways.

Jefferson: Many people speak of a god. I heard Pleiadians refer to it as prime Creator. I believe Bashar calls it All That Is. How do the Arkoreuns refer to the creator of all things?

Arvantis: Well, again, there is simply the idea we refer to as All That Is, which for us is the Creator of All That Is in all the different ways that it chooses to create its Isness. There are many different labels in different languages, even on your planet, which can be utilized to refer to All That Is.

Jefferson: Yeah.

Arvantis: All That Is exists within all life and is all life. It is in all of the races that are interacting in this moment with you and with all the people on your planet. You can learn to understand this better by getting a feeling of what All That Is is. To do so, perhaps lessen your focus on the term, the label, the name of All That Is, and begin to experience what All That Is is! Feel it more, thus then the heart that was "pulled out of the hat" can be then brought back magically into the embodiment of your physiological life and awareness there in your world so you can experience your heartfelt realities more fully once again with the Isness of All That Is. You can experience All That Is more fully in more heartfelt ways.

Jefferson: Hmm. Thank you! Arvantis, I was wandering if you can share with us anything in Arkoreun that you...something like, "good day," or...is that anything you could do?

Arvantis: You mean a phrase or a word in our language?

Jefferson: Yes!

Arvantis: Yes. One moment.

Jefferson: Thank you!

{...a brief moment of silence...}

Arvantis: Ahr in tor kai mor ren
Ahr in tor kai mor ren
Ahr in tor kai mor ren
Ahr in tor kai mor ren
Ahr in tor kai mor ren
Ahr in tor kai mor ren
Ahr in tor kai mor ren

Jefferson: Ahr in tor kai mor ren?

Arvantis: Ahr in tor kai mor ren

Jefferson: Ahr in tor kai mor ren?

Arvantis: Ahr in tor kai mor ren

Jefferson: Okay.

Arvantis: The translation is, "There is much love in our hearts for all of you!"

Jefferson: Wow. Can you help us with spelling?

Arvantis: That's not necessary. You will be able to put it together phonetically as you listen.

Jefferson: Sure! Wow! Thank you! So can you explain what took place during the silence that occurred just before you started speaking that phrase?

Arvantis: There were several factors involved. In a very light hearted sense, a consultation with the group here was taking place about what we wanted to share in that moment as we brought forth a language that has not been spoken on your world for some time. That is the idea then, a reintroduction of the language in words spoken for your world's vibratory frequency. There were also some variations in frequency that were necessary to make for the channel, (Shaun), slight adjustments so the channeling frequency would be able to flow through and bring forth that sound, that verbiage, that language. It contains certain wavelengths of feeling and understanding. It's not just words. There is much content underneath the words, within the words, within the vibration, as well.

Jefferson: And who is around there? Who is the group you refer to?

Arvantis: There are three groups present, and they are all of a genetically connected race with your society. That is all we can say at this time in those regards.

Jefferson: Oh come on, Arvantis!

Arvantis: But we thank you for your inquisitive enthusiasm!

Jefferson: Very good! And...ah...are you by the river again?

Arvantis: That is not my location. I am in a sphere, a craft that is something you would not see in your world if it was in the sky above you next to clouds, so to speak, for it is of a vibration a little bit beyond of your eyesight's capacity at this timing.

Jefferson: Okay.

Arvantis: And it is a large craft, very voluminous in size, several miles in size. But there are only approximately 15,000 people presently aboard. Most of them are focused in this communication at this timing, but not all of the 15,000. One, five, zero, zero, zero.

Jefferson: Wow! And they are from three different civilizations?

Arvantis: With a genetic connection to your society, yes, that is our present gathering status.

Jefferson: And what world is that? Is that your world?

Arvantis: One craft is a communal craft, and there are worlds others than ours, but that will not come through at this time.

Jefferson: Where are you? Where is this craft located?

Arvantis: It is near a world that is similar to your Earth, but it is at a frequency that would not be visible to your eyes if it was in your skies.

Jefferson: Oh!

Arvantis: But we are several thousands of miles beyond your present planet's surface.

Jefferson: Is that in my solar system?

Arvantis: Yes.

Jefferson: Oh, I know what you are doing...you are working on the postcard idea right?

Arvantis: Pictures from home!

Jefferson: Nah, I'm just kidding! So Arvantis, does anybody there have anything to say, or a question, or do you have any parting thoughts you would like to share?

Arvantis: There is only that it's a joy to interact with you! There is nothing, in that sense, that we feel we need to bring through. There isn't anything there that you are missing that we would have to fill you in on. We are certainly in a vibration of resonance with connecting and sharing in this way with you and those there. It is a great joy to do so! We thank you for this interaction in this way at this timing this day of your time!

Jefferson: Fantastic! So Arvantis, much love to you, to all the Arkoreuns, to everybody that is present in this timing and for those as well who will get in touch with this material at some point in time. I thank everybody for assisting and supporting us in any way they can. Much love to all of you and thank you!

Arvantis: Thank you, much love to you as well!

Jefferson: So I will see you soon Arvantis!

Arvantis: We look forward to this idea of communicating with you again as well!

Jefferson: Fantastic! Thank you!

Arvantis: Until then, thank you and good day!

Jefferson: Good day!

Chapter 10

Entering the 5th Dimension of Heart Vibrations

"We suggest there are foods that, when ingested, are more supportive of allowing a person to connect with who they really are. Foods that won't repress or "close the door" on their physiology's ability to tap into the fifth dimension, the heart frequency, the more expansive knowledge of their actual state of existence."

- Arvantis

March 30th, 2010

Arvantis: Most delightful to be here with you in these blending moments together in this day of your time! How are you?

Jefferson: Amazingly so! I am very excited to speak to you again!

Arvantis: And us as well! Thank you for choosing to move forward in this timing and to create experiences that can uplift your and our understanding. Thank you for choosing to explore more of the Infinite that we are in ways that we thoroughly enjoy! How would you enjoy exploring the Infinite in this moment together?

Jefferson: Are there parallel realities we can move into due to the type of choices we make?

Arvantis: You can only experience that reality of which you have chosen in terms of the personality that you perceive yourself to be. There are other aspects of you, in that sense, other personalities of you that then, if they are on a different reality, on a parallel reality, they have chosen that one.

Jefferson: So is there another Jefferson living a parallel reality on Earth?

Arvantis: Yes!

Jefferson: How many?

Arvantis: There are a few hundred at this timing!

Jefferson: Wow! So every choice takes us somewhere, and a choice made by a parallel self will probably have a different ending than the choice I make?

Arvantis: Yes!

Jefferson: So let's say there is a parallel reality where another Jefferson has made a great discovery and contributed immensely to the planet. Is there any possibility that I could jump into that reality by shifting my vibration and start existing there?

Arvantis: It is possible!

Jefferson: Did you say there are other Jeffersons living in parallel realities?

Arvantis: Yes.

Jefferson: Is the same Arvantis that is talking to me, talking to another parallel Jefferson?

Arvantis: That is the idea, yes.

Jefferson: Okay. And how is his life turning out?

Arvantis: Very well, perfectly as that one is choosing for it to be.

Jefferson: Has he met you personally as well?

Arvantis: There have been a few occasions of that type of meeting, yes!

Jefferson: When was the first time you met an extraterrestrial, physically?

Arvantis: I was born in a group of extraterrestrials.

Jefferson: Where?

Arvantis: On planet Revision 5.

Jefferson: Who are those other extraterrestrials that were with you on your world when you were born?

Arvantis: There were several that would not be in your vocabulary at this timing. They are of a different physiological form. They are not what you would consider a humanoid. They are not of a two leg, two arm, a head, a torso, type of physiology.

Jefferson: Oh, okay. How many languages do you speak?

Arvantis: I have this one that I grew up with, that is a part of my society. There are others that I can understand on a deeper level of communication such that it isn't necessary for me to learn each society's language. There is an underlying language that I speak that, in a sense, translates internally with that other society so they can understand me as though I was speaking their language. When they speak their language, it is as though they were speaking my language, in terms of how I perceive what they are saying. It is as though there is a built-in translator that takes effect.

Jefferson: On Earth we have a popular movie about an extraterrestrial race that lives on a planet called Pandora. The people in that movie have light blue skin like yours. Do you know what I am talking about?

Arvantis: Yes!

Jefferson: Okay. Is there a society that is like the one in that movie?

Arvantis: There are a few in our experience that are only somewhat like that.

Jefferson: In what ways is your society different from that one?

Arvantis: We do not go to war for any occasion! We do not have conflict in any instance with any of those other forms of life in our existence, in our region, in our physical worlds.

Jefferson: Okay. What about physiological differences?

Arvantis: There are a variety of physiological variations that occur. Size, shapes, colors. These are all opportunities for variations to come through, to come forth. There are far too many to enumerate in this hour of session timing together today.

Jefferson: Oh. So you are saying there are a lot of differences between the Arkoreuns and the society in that blockbuster movie, too many to mention now?

Arvantis: More than we have interest in focusing upon. Our world is of great harmony. The characters in that movie live in a world that is still cast in shadow and conflict, but that allows your society to receive particular messages that are in resonance with your society's present state of choice. That movie is appropriate as a story for your society to be taking a part in by viewing and experiencing the ideas it presents.

Jefferson: And in your understanding, is there a society that is exactly like that one that actually exists?

Arvantis: Not in our understanding, but there certainly could be.

Jefferson: On Earth, we are living at a time where we are experiencing unprecedented changes in all avenues of life. What can you share with us about these changes that we are going

through?

Arvantis: There is the consciousness that is coming together with its heart. More people are allowing this frequency of heart feeling and sensation to flow within their awareness so it can be a part of their life. In that way, to explore this fifth dimension. To get into the heart frequency. At this frequency, feelings such as being upset are absent from your experiences in life. People at this heart frequency, this fifth dimension, are free from discordance, free from depression, free from the sadness, free from tears of pain, simply because those old ways are, in a sense, corrupted with frequencies of misaligned thought regarding the actual nature of life.

There is in this time of awakening an ability for your society to connect more to the heart, to this fifth dimension, to feeling that which is more in alignment with your actual nature. And to feel that which is more true, more whole, that which is clear of sad, pain, and depression. For again, those discordant feelings are convoluted and conflicted with thoughts that are out of alignment with who you all truly are.

Thus then, the changes are numerous in your society at this time. There are so many old constructs your world has created that have been preventing the ability to connect with this heart frequency. Because you choose now to begin connecting more with the heart frequency, all of those old constructs that had been keeping you from connecting to the heart frequency have to unwind. They have to unfold. They have to come down. They have to be dismantled. They have to be a frequency that you will no longer find desirable to be focusing in, swimming in. And this is going to create large shifts in all aspects of your society.

The infrastructure of your world: the political systems, the educational systems, the medical systems, the science systems, the health systems, the family systems, all of these are changing and will continue to do so until you're more in alignment with who you are and then allowing for the heart feeling frequency to come forth. A fifth dimension can then be more present in your awareness.

The changes that occur will be varied and will be frequent. At times it will be quite chaotic for some, but then you are learning to make the adjustments without too much chaos, without too much fear being brought to the surface, without too much crumbling. You are finding ways to dismantle the old infrastructures rather than to wreak havoc. This is a process that will take many years of your society's time to create this dismantling and thus then create more ways to support this fifth dimension, this heart frequency of conscious beings. It is a choice your society, in our perception presently, is choosing to make. Gradually, this shift is coming forth. Changes will continue for some time!

Jefferson: When you say, "changes will continue for some time," how many years are we looking at?

Arvantis: Decades, several decades of your timing.

Jefferson: Hmm. Wow! Are there other extraterrestrials around you now?

Arvantis: We have presently three societies of which one would be the Sassani society. The other would be that which would be similar to the Yahyel society, and there is then our own for the third, in that sense, three, present.

Jefferson: Are you in the same ship you were last time?

Arvantis: I am presently aboard a craft that is somewhat like the other one but not as large. This one is more of a cigar shape. But again, it is very much of an etheric quality, not of a crafted metallic structure that you have on your world.

Jefferson: And why are you there?

Arvantis: For the experiences that are most moving and enjoyable for me to be present.

Jefferson: Are you studying biology with these people? Are you teaching, learning?

Arvantis: There is some opportunity for that to occur, yes, and sharing in that way does take place.

Jefferson: I want to know more about your adventures to other worlds and the things you see. The people you meet, their habits,

their societal structures.

Arvantis: There is a society that is known as the Rorkins that you perhaps have heard of.

Jefferson: Yes!

Arvantis: We were upon a craft and we interacted with them briefly. In that interaction, they were able to show us some of their agriculture that they had been planting for some time. There was, in that sense, a new form of food that they had received from the Yahyel as a gift. It was a plant of a green bean food. The Rorkins are like gardeners, farmers. But they were cultivating that food on a planet that was new to them. It was a planet that they discovered through the guidance of the Yahyel who took them there for the purpose of planting this new leafy green bean food.

The Rorkins showed us how they have been able to build a very large farm of this green bean food that has enabled them to provide the sustenance, this form of food, for other civilizations that were not necessarily in need of food, but were excited to have this new food form brought forth to them. This food has adjusted within their consciousness and understanding in such a way that their awareness ability within them has actually expanded. They are more intuitive in ways that they find very amazing, very uplifting. And it is, they realize, a result of this new form of food that they have welcomed into their societies that the Rorkins brought forth to them.

Once every three revolutions of their planet around its Sun, the Rorkins always are in great delight as they have a meal as a ceremony for this food and as a form of appreciation for having this gift been brought forth from the Yahyel to them. They are then in that way expressing their gratitude for having received that gift.

They are able to make new worldly creations of experience and manifest new ideas on their planet as a result of the doorways, if you will, of imagination that have been opened from the energy frequency contained within the food, the leafy green bean food.

We share this so you may know that food can have an immense impact, an immense supportive capacity for your understanding of yourself and your world in your ability to imagine more fully and to create more joyful realities. The frequency of the food that you take in to your body can have an enormous effect upon you.

You can also consider how foods that are so highly processed in your world might impact you in ways that close "worlds of imagination" and, in that sense, close off opportunities for you to connect to more of your real nature, that restrict your ability to sense your heart frequency more fully.

That then is one idea we share for you of how humans from another world have had a food impact them so wonderfully. How a food had expanded, and nourished, and enriched their perception of their existence.

Jefferson: What can you tell us about the society in the ship that is close in appearance to the Yahyel?

Arvantis: They are, in a sense, cousins of the Yahyel. They are quite similar. They have a different planet, but they have a close bond with the Yahyel.

Jefferson: Hmm.

Arvantis: They are in constant contact.

Jefferson: Okay. Arvantis, have you ever met a Pleiadian person?

Arvantis: I have met a being that perhaps your society would consider a Pleiadian, but there are other names, other terminologies that we do not see any need to bring forth at this time. What then brings forth the curiosity from you to ask the question?

Jefferson: Are you asking why?

Arvantis: Yes!

Jefferson: It is one of the societies that we most hear of on our planet, the Pleiadians. So I was wondering, since you travel so much, if the Pleiadians are one of the societies that look closer in appearance to us other than the Yahyel?

Arvantis: There are some in a region that you could perceive as being in that Pleiadian region of your skies at night. They are quite similar to your genetic humanoid physiological creation-ship, the craft you call your body!

Jefferson: What about the Pleiadian you met?

Arvantis: There are several from that region that I have interacted with. You could say they are Pleiadians, but they would not necessarily apply that terminology to themselves. They would understand why your society would, for they then are in an area of space that you consider a Pleiadian region.

Jefferson: You once said that we visited a region of Arcturus. Could you expand on that idea? Why would I prefer to go there?

Arvantis: You were there for a transition into your physical life here on Earth. There were some adjustments of frequency. It was like a learning ground for you but not so much that you were studying to learn. Simply that you were becoming acquainted with, acclimated with, certain frequencies, certain ideologies that existed on Earth, certain concepts and constructs of physical manifestation that occur on Earth. You were in the Arcturus region to make the adjustments to feel more acclimated. Do you understand that idea?

Jefferson: To feel more acclimated to what?

Arvantis: To Earth!

Jefferson: How so?

Arvantis: To align you with the frequency most in alignment with what you are presently experiencing yourself to be. The ideas that excite you. The endeavors you choose to pursue, and so on and so forth.

Jefferson: And the beings on that planet, are they humanoid?

Arvantis: There are a few that are what you could call humanoid, but they are very much of a non physical quality in terms of what you can consider physical. They are quite a different frequency.

Jefferson: They are more evolved?

Arvantis: They generally have a more expansive perspective and understanding of Existence.

Jefferson: What reality is there now on Earth as far as extraterrestrial beings coming and going?

Arvantis: There are a wide variety of interactions that take place on an ongoing basis with your Earth's spacious planet. Yes, quite a bit of activity!

Jefferson: So if I wanted to go and study with you guys for two weeks, would that be possible?

Arvantis: There will be a time perhaps but not presently. Not in the idea the way you are thinking. Not like we would lift you up on a craft and you would then go somewhere. That perhaps could happen at some point but not presently.

Jefferson: You mean at some point when open contact with the Yahyel has occurred?

Arvantis: There is that as a possibility, yes.

Jefferson: So the Yahyel might be one of the first human ET societies to contact us peacefully in public. Who else will be a part of the early open and public contacts with us?

Arvantis: There are various possibilities in terms of timing and who will be coming first or second and so on and so forth. There are also possibilities that several could present themselves simultaneously.

Jefferson: Oh.

Arvantis: These are ideas and realities that then will come through in the time that they occur. There are several ideas possible and your world's collective consciousness is taking part in deciding, along with those extraterrestrials. How it will come forth is a collective choice that will be made amongst your world and those worlds of the extraterrestrials making the initial peaceful and public contacts.

Jefferson: You said before that we would feel quite different in your presence if you were to be here and talk to us. Could you comment on that?

Arvantis: There is quite a different frequency of consciousness that we embody and that then would have an impact upon you. As an analogy, your moon has an impact upon the tides and the oceans. There then is a type of consciousness within that field of energy of the moon that has an impact upon your planet's ocean and tides. There is a gravity present within our beingness and consciousness, for gravity is a type of consciousness. Planetary gravity is also a type of consciousness. There is then in our beingness a form of gravitational consciousness that would have an impact upon your Earth beings and there would be then in your physiology, the oceans of your biologies, some tidal changes taking place. This would have an impact in several different ways. Some relating to the physiological sensations of your biology and then also in terms of the mind and your ability to perceive from one moment to the next, and what you are feeling from one moment to the next.

All of these ideas are based on consciousness which then has a quality potentially of gravitational flux that we then would have an influence upon if we were physically next to you. You would have changes in your thought patterns, in your feeling patterns, and also how you perceive your body sensations. Those different sensations, different feelings, and thoughts, would be varied from one to the next.

Jefferson: We have met before. How has my biology responded to those meetings?

Arvantis: Your body was in what you could call an energetic cocoon that, with your willingness, we placed around you so the effect would be not quite the same as we were referring to before. But there is still some influence upon you that you do carry back with you when you come back on your planet's surface.

You have different feelings, sensations, and thoughts to some degree that allow you to resonate more with things that are more open, more real, more in tune and in alignment with the way existence actually is. That then allows you to open doors more easily that are more filled with experiences you find to be exciting for you, vibrant for you.

Jefferson: And how do you place this field around my body?

Arvantis: That then is something we could not explain. You would not have vocabulary to understand it and this is necessary so you can exist in a world like you do where there is such a predominant idea that it isn't possible to even do such a thing to begin with. So that would be a foreign language for us to describe it.

Jefferson: I was wondering...do you have technology to beam something from your world to my world?

Arvantis: That is something that could be done yes.

Jefferson: And could you, for example, instantly beam the postcard to me?

Arvantis: That is possible.

Jefferson: Why don't we do this with something?

Arvantis: Why would you like to do that?

Jefferson: To have something from your world!

Arvantis: What is it that you find so exciting about that activity?

Jefferson: Oh, because having something from another world...it seems to me to be an exciting thing! Like...like...you know, what is that thing that you wear on your neck?

Arvantis: I don't at this timing have that on my body, but what is it about having something that you find so exciting?

Jefferson: Why? Because...when I have such a thing around my neck...it is almost like a...

Arvantis: You would wear a postcard around your neck?

Jefferson: No...I am talking about the amulet!

Arvantis: Very well.

Jefferson: I just mentioned the postcard as an example.

Arvantis: And why would you like us to do that?

Jefferson: Because I would have some souvenir from you.

Arvantis: Perhaps you could craft an amulet with us in mind as you design it and put it together. In that way, you could have a remembrance of us.

Jefferson: Yes but there is a lot of excitement in having it to come from another planet!

Arvantis: Very well.

Jefferson: So let's do this!

Arvantis: In appropriate timing, yes!

Jefferson: Appropriate timing is after 2012?

Arvantis: Perhaps!

Jefferson: Okay. What are the colors of your seven moons?

Arvantis: Those are primarily going to be a secret!

Jefferson: You said some of you live in the forests of your planet, Revision 5, but you have not spoken about your cities. What can you tell us today about your cities?

Arvantis: We don't really have cities.

Jefferson: Oh...you don't have pavement?

Arvantis: This is something we don't have.

Jefferson: Do you wear shoes?

Arvantis: We can wear things that would be like a shoe that would be of our planet's organic production.

Jefferson: Are there any forms of life on your world that would be able to live on another planet such as Earth?

Arvantis: There are some of those ideas that have made that transition successfully onto your planet.

Jefferson: Can you give some examples?

Arvantis: Not at this time. But it is something you have seen before in your nature, in the outdoors, nature.

Jefferson: How do you work out your lighting system, electrical installations? Do you have this on your planet?

Arvantis: Not in the way you have a network of wires, no.

Jefferson: In what sense do you have, if you do?

Arvantis: We are able to interact on our world in ways that don't require us to have light bulbs and don't require us to have televisions, or stoves, or refrigerators. So we don't have a requirement for wires in order to access the energy, the energy that is already present in our space. We have an understanding of how to focus on energy that is of luminary potential for us to bring forth a light, in a sense, if it is night and we want to have light.

We can produce an illumination of light that would work similar to a light bulb on your world, but it isn't necessary to have wires because we access that which is also present on your world, a form of the nature of existence that is always teaming with life energy. Always able to be, in a sense, tapped into. In that sense, it is free energy. In that sense, we do not have to create a structure of companies and networks of grids that then can control whether, and when, and how much energy we have access to.

The energy is infinite, and it is present, and we understand how to access those portions of it that are a joy and support us in our physiological functioning on our planet. There are numerous ways to access this infinite free energy that we haven't even begun to tap into.

But presently on our world, we tap into those forms of this energy that we enjoy and that provide us with that which is fulfilling for us.

Jefferson: You said your age on your world is approximately seventy-three and on ours it is about one-third of that. I think one-third of seventy-three is about twenty-five. Is that your age on Earth?

Arvantis: We gave you some approximate ideas of our ages so you would have a foundation to relate to us from. And those ideas we will put to rest for now so that you can begin building relationships in other areas with other topics that we feel would be more enriching and revealing of your nature and of the relationship you have with extraterrestrial societies so you aren't going around focusing on ages, in that sense. Those are all ideas that will be brought forth as the physical contact develops more fully in the decades to come. Those are all ideas that will flush themselves out more readily as our societies have more time to interact with your society face to face, heart to heart. Those are all, in a sense, surface concepts. There are more integral, more foundational ideas that we can bring forth presently in this timing before that timing when we make physical, open, peaceful, contact to help awaken Earth's awareness.

There are deeper more foundational ideas that your society will require, in a sense, to understand before so much of the tiny details, in a sense, can be brought forth. But we thank you for being curious about such details.

Jefferson: Can you speak of one foundational idea that our society would be uplifted by in the present as we progress —

Arvantis: There is then the idea that we spoke of with the Yahyel and Rorkins having shared the food that allowed it to expand its imagination, simply from consuming that food. So your society can understand that eating more organic or whole food — less processed food — isn't just about getting more healthy. It's about allowing your body and physiology to become more tuned in to your actual whole nature so you can connect more with the fifth dimensional heart feeling frequency.

In that sense, that is a very fundamental understanding that most in your world have no way to even grasp at this timing, to even consider as a possibility, or a reality at this timing. For they are so disconnected from the understanding of what ingesting forms of food can do to their sense of beingness, to their ability to connect to self-realization and to be more in a space that is in alignment with infinite ecstasy and joy. That is a very powerful fundamental understanding that we feel your society would be very positively uplifted by to learn, to experience, to appreciate, to acknowledge, to teach, to understand, to realize, to embrace. Do you follow that idea?

Jefferson: Would you suggest then that the idea of being vegetarian is more conducive than otherwise?

Arvantis: We suggest there are foods that, when ingested, are more supportive of allowing a person to connect with who they really are. Foods that won't repress or "close the door" on their physiology's ability to tap into the fifth dimension, the heart frequency, the more expansive knowledge of their actual state of existence.

There are many foods that are very heavily processed that will, in a sense, numb out the ability of a person to tap into who they really are, or to even accept the idea that the life they are living is disconnected from an awareness of who they really are. Your society doesn't have to become vegetarian, but there are more vegetable foods that are more supportive for the physiology to connect to more of its heart nature than there are processed foods.

In our present awareness, almost all processed foods are something that would be far more likely to numb out the physiology. Not all, but most. Whereas most vegetables would be in a place to support and open up the physiology's ability to connect to more of its heart nature.

It is for each person to choose if they want then to have more vegetables and to open up more, or to remain in a state of numbness and choose more processed foods. It is always a choice. However, given that frequencies are such as they are, a person cannot continue to resonate at a processed heavy-frequency of darkness — that which is a frequency of limited ideas — and expect then to connect to more of their heart's whole, joyful, fully abundant nature. You can't have both because loving frequencies and, in that sense, rejecting frequencies, repel one another.

Jefferson: Okay. Since we are not making a list of foods for this

book, would you suggest that people can follow their intuition? How will people know what is better for them to do?

Arvantis: To simply choose that which they feel is most uplifting for them to do, that they are able to do.

Jefferson: So it is about doing what you can, not more and not less?

Arvantis: In each moment, do that which is most enjoyable for you that you are able to do! You do not have to quantify it with right or wrong, or do more or less of this. Simply, as best you can in each moment, do that which you are able to that is most uplifting for you to do. As simple as that! You do not need to place any quantification upon it.

Jefferson: Do the laws that we have in our legal systems around the world impact the timing of when we will have peaceful and public contact with your society?

Arvantis: Many of your countries do have laws that make it illegal, in terms of how your society defines the idea of legal and illegal, many countries have laws that make it illegal for the citizens to have contact with extraterrestrial life.

And while many of those laws are written in vague terms, they are written in vague terms to encompass all forms of extraterrestrial life. Not just biological, microbial extraterrestrial life, but also intelligent, loving, and peaceful extraterrestrial societies as well. Those laws were written by people at a timing when it was known by those writers that there are loving and wise extraterrestrial beings.

So let your world become more aware of these laws that, in a sense, lessen our ability to contact you and your society. Become aware that these laws are, in a sense, on the books and then pass new laws that say you are, as citizens of each country, open to having open, peaceful, loving contact with extraterrestrial life forms. That will go a long way in allowing extraterrestrials to make contact with you.

For as long as it is illegal on your world to contact us, we will honor your laws and remain removed from the citizens of your countries so that you then will not be placed in a situation that your authorities would have to enforce the laws if you were to have contact with us. We will not put you in a position of being called out as someone who has violated the law by having contact with us. We will remain removed from your public's physical sight in terms of physical contact until your countries choose to make it legally acceptable.

There are individual contacts that take place privately and they, in this sense, are a different matter.

Also, until your world as a collective understands sufficiently its actual nature, there will not be a strong enough frequency of vibrational resonance for our extraterrestrial societies to have open, peaceful contact with yours, for the vibrational frequencies would be too different.

Jefferson: Oh.

Arvantis: So then, we suggest you focus more on the fundamental ideas of your actual nature and the nature and structure of Existence. Understand those sooner, thus then sooner the contact can occur. From our perspective, making lists of numerous details about us such as dates, and names, and labels of various sorts are, in a sense, preventing a person from focusing more on the fundamental ideas.

Jefferson: Very well Arvantis. What are your parting thoughts tonight?

Arvantis: We thank you for the time, the questions, the sharings, the blendings. We look forward to having with you one more of these interchanges. At that timing it will be, in a sense, a final chapter to this initial book that you have been so wonderful in choosing to author and co-create with us. And there is an opportunity before that next channeling, for you to put forth ideas that you would like to sum up from any material brought forth in the prior chapters, the prior channeling sessions that we have had.

Jefferson: Sure!

Arvantis: There will be guidance if you ask in your dream states, in your awake states, of questions, of sharings that you would like to have in that final session. Thus then, you need only ask that those ideas be brought into your awareness to help you bring forth the material for that session. Do you understand this idea?

Jefferson: Yes! I do.

Arvantis: Thank you.

Jefferson: I do!

Arvantis: And you? Any parting thoughts that you would like to share?

Jefferson: I thank you very much for also taking the time and sharing your understandings, and your ideas, and you are always so excited...it always seems that every interchange is brand new for you. I thank you very much for your enthusiasm and for the emotion that you give us through your personality. You are always motivated to talk to us. You are always happy, in that sense, sharing ideas with us. So I thank you very much for that!

Arvantis: Thank you for sharing! Wonderful to hear you expressing much joy through those ideas. Until we have the opportunity to blend with you in this way again dear one, much love to you and good day!

Jefferson: Much love to you Arvantis, thank you very much!

Chapter 11

Smiling in the Mirror of Physical Reality

"In time, as more people have this awakening, there will become a strong enough vibration on your planet to hold connection with our society and other extraterrestrial societies so we can have open, peaceful contact with you on your planet face to face, heart to heart."

- Arvantis

April 6th, 2010

Arvantis: Wonderful to be in this timing, in this experience of blending and having this opportunity to share with you! How are you?

Jefferson: Fantastic, thank you! How are you?

Arvantis: Lovely! Thank you for taking the time to step in this place of exploration of our world, and your world, and of the infinite that we are. In this way we can share, and explore, and unveil, and review more of this information for others to find and to be open to more of who they are, to find more of their fascination and their joy, to find more of the wisdom and knowledge and intelligence that they too can be the architects of a life that is for them practical and also filled with laughter and free from sadness. Filled with joy and free from fear. Full of vitality and absent of all depression.

Information such as this that we bring forth together can help, can be a catalyst for those who read this information and hear of this information to more readily connect to this state of reality in which they are more in alignment with who they really are. That state of joy and laughter, and wisdom, and knowledge, and absence of depression, and fear, and sadness. They can fully step aside from those illusions, those misperceptions, those theatrical plays that are out of alignment with the actual state of every human being on planet Earth's real state of existence. So how are you?

Jefferson: Some people say that the systems on Earth are corrupt, that they don't work, they don't support life, and they don't support the planet. Some people suggest that systems such as money, military, media, and religion control everybody and everything. From your perspective, who is to blame? Can you tell us if this is all just a reflection of the collective's choices or is it the result of unfair evil people working behind the curtains, so to speak?

Arvantis: It is a choice your collective society has made to live in a state of, if you will, darkness, a place in which they feel there is a limitation on who they are, a place in which they feel they must do and follow certain deeds or else they will be sent to an eternal purgatory. There is a great deal of collective choice that is made before people are incarnated, before they are into that place of physical birthing, physical embodiment in a physiological body.

Many people stay focused in the vibration of consciousness that contains this limitation in order then that they can have an experience of this limited or "dark" state of being. There are many reasons why your collective society has chosen to explore this "dark game," this disconnected state of being.

You could say there are people behind governments that are evil, but that isn't their actual state of being. They are simply playing those parts and, for the most part, they are still hidden from your population's awareness. For many people still don't accept that there are shadow governments or people behind the scenes that are influencing the direction of your collective consciousness and, in a sense, keeping it in a state of darkness in which so many people aren't willing to accept that there is more to who they are, and people aren't yet willing to accept they are the creators of their reality. So you could say there are evil people behind the scenes in military, and economic, and governmental systems of your world, but again, they are just playing parts in order to carry out the overall "play of limitation and darkness."

Now, your society is collectively choosing to come back and remember more of its actual state of infinite creatorship being. More people are awakening. Awareness is increasing. The age of awareness and awakening is gathering strength and momentum around the world as more people begin to choose to wake up and see who they really are. In doing that, those who are behind the scenes, perhaps thought of as evil, will begin to be brought into the light. And more awakening people will begin to say, "we don't want that hidden control structure anymore, that type of limited system. We want to become a world that provides for everyone lovingly and abundantly in positive ways." So you will begin gradually seeing your world shift into a place where all humans have all they need, all in the sense of energy, money, food, shelter, and education in the ways that are of most deliciousness for their state of desire.

So it is a process of change, and it has begun, and the momentum is of such strength that it will not be stopped. There may be a few hiccups here and there along the way, a few minor obstacles, but the end result will be that your world will be one as a collective that is aware and functioning more in alignment with your whole nature as creators of your world. Everyone will have attained the ability to know thyself and to be fear free, and to be fully in alignment with joy, and to be aware of their infinite nature. So there will no longer be any possibility for the shadow, controlling, manipulative types to have a place on your world.

Jefferson: Thank you!

Arvantis: Would you like to explore that further or does that answer your question?

Jefferson: For now that will do superbly! Are there beliefs or attitudes that people have that perhaps are not in their best service to have or be putting out?

Arvantis: Well, a person limits their self if they choose to hold on to the old idea of separation and limitation that their creator is outside of them. Generally, such a person is living in fear and not willing to step into their true creatorship, not willing to stand in the light and say, "I am a Creator and this is what I prefer, this is what I enjoy!" Many people are not yet willing to do that. They are still wanting to hide, in a sense, and be part of the flock, if you will, a flock of sheep where they won't step out of line in any way. They do this because they are feeling fear from believing the illusory ideas that suggest they will be cast out or laughed at if they step away from the old belief that humans are separate from God, from true Creator. Their fears are very powerful.

To make the adjustment away from the old idea of separation from one's Creator, people can become more comfortable with who they really are and know that will support them. They can step out and express their true self more fully and that vibration will be supported more fully now in the new consciousness that's awakening on your planet.

Jefferson: Yeah!

Arvantis: And they will not be cast out! They will not be laughed at in any way that lessens their experience of who they really are. So as more people in that way simply follow their heart, and speak out, and share, and express their true creatorship and creativity, over time the vibrations in that way will become so strong that the old ideas and those old vibrations of limitation and fear will begin to subside. The old ideas will begin to lose their power, in a sense, to frighten people, to cause people to go back in a shell, like a turtle hiding within and not willing to put its head out.

People on your world are still hiding within their shell and not ready and willing to put their head out and say this is who I am. I am a loving being, and I prefer to do this. Many people are still doing things they don't really enjoy. They are still following the flock. They are still feeling they have to go to work at a 9 to 5 job that they don't enjoy.

In time as more people follow their heart, get in touch with their heart, these old ways and infrastructures will fall gradually. The transitions will be made in your system and in society's infrastructure so it will support everyone's coming into the light of who they really are so that each person can then be as productive as they are capable of being in a way that is in alignment with their heart, their wisdom, their knowledge. Your true intelligence as individuals will then be supported simply by following your heart and not hiding within the shell of the current limiting social and economic structural systems.

Jefferson: Do you think the mass consciousness has somehow an impact on the choices a person makes?

Arvantis: There are many people who tune in to the mass consciousness channel and then it is in that place they determine who they are. That is where they go to get their identity. They look outside of themselves, in a sense, to determine who they should be and what they should be doing. Only by going within and finding their inner channel will they come into contact with who they really are, and what they are most capable of expressing, and how they are capable of being most productive from connecting within to their individual channel. And then they will let go of the mass consciousness's current frequency or channel that is based in limitation, and fear, and separation.

Jefferson: Do you think our society is free?

Arvantis: There is within all of you a freedom of eternal, infinite potential. But your collective consciousness has created an illusory world where there is great deal of limitation that is like shackles on your minds. The shackles are like chains upon your creativity. In that way, a large percentage of you are in a *prison cell* of your own choice. A choice that is made on a deeper level of your consciousness, so that you could come onto this planet and experience limitation. In a sense, you have chosen to be in a *cell* in which there are limitations and lack of awareness of who you really are.

Following your heart is the key that will allow you to unlock the *prison cell door* so that you may then emerge and begin experiencing your actual infinite freedom in various exciting and enticing ways!

Jefferson: So what would you suggest to people that are willing to follow their heart but are still exposed each day to this mass consciousness that is so deeply focused on limitation, and separation from their Creator, and also focused on systems that don't honor life?

Arvantis: To simply follow your heart in the best way you can. If you feel like sharing ideas that are exciting for you to do, then step in that way. If there are those who aren't willing or interested in listening, allow them to be who they choose, and then find those who are willing to make the change, willing to become more whole and to connect to more of their true knowledge, their true wisdom, their true ability to manifest in your physical world experiences that are most in alignment with their actual nature that will be of great support for them.

So simply find topics to talk about in public places that people have been invited to attend. Those who attend, if they are willing to step forward, they will do so. If there are those who aren't interested, they will move along. For those who might try and create resistance to you, you can simply let them be. And you can simply find another location at which to present your material again to new attendees and some returning attendees as well.

Jefferson: Okay.

Arvantis: There are more and more places opening up in public settings that are welcoming people to present valuable information.

Jefferson: Thank you very much Arvantis. What can you say for people that think, "what I love to do, what my heart tells me to do, doesn't seem to be able to support me financially?"

Arvantis: They aren't yet accepting their actual nature. People are infinitely supported in whatever way they choose to believe they can be supported in. You are infinite beings. You exist infinitely. When you choose to recognize you are of infinite joy, recognize that is your actual state of being, and you allow yourself to be more in that state of being, then it gives the infinite Universe more opportunity to find ways to support you in your choice to be more an expression of the actual joyful and infinitely abundant person you are. "What you put out is what you get back."

You are infinitely abundant, infinitely supported, infinitely joyful, and when you act as that, it makes it easier for the Universe to find you and to bring forth opportunities that will provide you that financial support. But it is important that the person actually accepts that, believes that, puts that out so they then can get back that reality.

There are people who make this attempt to follow their heart, but because they don't truly believe doing so will support them financially, they get back experiences that, in a sense, shut them down, in a sense, prevent them from attaining the idea they had been originally working to accomplish. They simply didn't believe that they could do what they most enjoyed and also be supported financially by doing it. And thus, because they didn't fully believe it would work, that then is what they put out, and so they got back experiences that, in a sense, short-circuited their efforts.

Believe that you are worthy of being financially supported when you are following your heart, "put out" that type of abundance, and you will allow the Universe to then "bring back" that reality.

Jefferson: So maybe it would help to take small steps at a time and not expect too much too soon?

Arvantis: Yes.

Jefferson: Maybe...don't walk away from a job that supports you financially and expect, "I am going to follow my heart and be immediately supported financially." Perhaps it takes time for a person to truly change their belief structure and fully accept this idea? So basically, take small steps until you feel comfortable to fly?

Arvantis: Well, going a step at a time can be most beneficial for most people. That is a good approach.

Jefferson: What is the best set of attitudes a person can engage in, in order to stay on Earth and participate smoothly in the transition that Earth is going through right now?

Arvantis: Well, in a sense, to know they are an infinite being. They are ecstasy infinitely. They are supported eternally. They are the creator of their reality. They are connected to all life. What they put out then is what they get back. These are attitudes, in a sense, ideas to have in their aware state of being on a daily basis. And they will even find it beneficial to write these ideas down and then read them several times each day.

They are an infinite being of infinite ecstasy, of infinite potential, infinite opportunity, infinitely exciting activities they can undergo at any given moment. What they put out is what they get back. They are the creator of their reality. Everybody always make choices to do what they perceive is closest to pleasure and farthest from pain.

Have these attitudes within their awareness, several times, everyday, throughout the day. Revisit these ideas several times consciously, to "put that out." Thus then you will "get back" experiences confirming and supporting that recognition, that understanding of their actual creator nature. By doing this, there will then be an ever expanding understanding of how to build new attitudes that will support this idea even further.

You will become more in tune to who you really are. You become more productive and feel that you are being fully productive in each moment, as fully as you need to be! You will feel that you are being of greatest service in each moment, no matter how small your actions may seem to be to others.

When you follow your heart in each moment, you are being of greatest service to All That Is as best you can be in your current physical incarnation. As you accept this, there will then be more experiences coming into your awareness of why this is so, how this is so, how fulfilling it is to make this simple acknowledgement within yourself to realize the truth, the magnitude of the beauty in that. Following your heart is the way you can be of greatest service. The more you put that out the more you will experience it and the more deeply you will understand why that is so.

Jefferson: Some people say—

Arvantis: Most people simply aren't willing to do this, to have these attitudes. They give up too quickly, and they get back in the consciousness of the flock, of the limitation, of the channel of consciousness that keeps playing reruns of *limitation programs* such as, "if you live on Earth, you have to have fear of something. You have to be frightened of something. You have to have some sadness. You have to have some depression. And occasionally you have to feel hurt by something." These are all ideas that are inaccurate in terms of your true potential, in terms of who you really are. It is time for your society to begin to walk away from those belittling concepts that are just misperceptions of your actual nature.

Jefferson: I see. So some say you have to monitor your thoughts and to —

Arvantis: It can help to be aware of what you are thinking. You don't have to monitor them.

Jefferson: Yeah. So if we are engaged in an activity that feels bad, what we have to do in self-honesty is to stop doing that and start looking for things that bring us joy?

Arvantis: All energy is one energy. It is infinite ecstasy. When you have your belief system in alignment with this understanding, you will feel good. If you have a feeling that it is not good, then you've chosen a thought, a belief, that is out of alignment with your true self and thus then you are getting back, instead of ecstasy, something that is out of alignment with ecstasy. It feels bad. Your thought is out of alignment with your true nature. Your belief system has a discordant definition.

Feeling bad is the result of flowing your true ecstasy through a misaligned thought, a belief system that is out of alignment with your true nature. Become aware of that. If you feel bad, then recognize that you have a thought that is out of alignment with your true state of being. Let the thought, the belief, come forth in your awareness. Recognize it as being out of alignment and change it to a thought that allows you to experience being more in alignment with who you really are. Change the thought, change the belief, redefine.

You don't need to uncover the details within every belief that is out of alignment. It can be enough if you simply recognize when you are feeling bad that you must have a belief about something that is out of alignment with your true self. Tell yourself you want to bring that discordant belief back into alignment so you can then feel more of the ecstasy that is your true nature. It can be this simple. That can be enough to realign that discordant thought back into alignment with your actual state of beingness.

Remember, re-awaken, experience in each moment that you are infinite, that you are ecstasy, that you are the one who creates your reality.

These are the ideas and attitudes to be more aware of every day. Remember these attitudes and ideas each day. Keep them in your thoughts.

Jefferson: Okay!

Arvantis: You don't need to take inventory on every thought that runs through your mind. That isn't something that is required. The more you focus on these attitudes that are in alignment with your true nature, the fewer chaotic thoughts you will have circulating in your mind. You will be more at peace and be with calm thoughts. You will have thoughts in each moment that are comforting and supporting, wise, intelligent, and brilliant. They will reveal more of your actual loving nature to you in ways you will be excited about!

Jefferson: How do we keep ourselves positive and looking forward when religion is telling us we are sinners and the money system says we are worthless, and the military says we will do as they say?

Arvantis: Again, you focus on yourself. As an analogy, if you were standing in front of a mirror and you see your reflection before you and you want your reflection to smile, you don't go up to the mirror and start trying to change your reflection in the glass into a smile. So you don't go out into your society and start trying to manipulate the military, or the religions, or the economic financial systems. If you want to see a smile on the reflection in the mirror, you have to smile first. Only then can the reflection in the mirror smile back at you. If you want your military, religious, economic, and financial systems to change, you have to change first. It cannot work any other way. Each person is responsible for making their own inner changes within themselves. You must smile first before the mirror, the reflection, will smile. You must find your value first before the external market place will begin to acknowledge your value!

Jefferson: It makes sense!

Arvantis: You must find it within yourself to govern yourself internally before your government will begin to acknowledge you are self governing and that policing is no longer necessary, and that military is no longer necessary. It is necessary for you to find your connection into the infinite source of Creation before your religions are willing to give you the reigns by saying, "all right, you are the true godship Creator." It must come from within. You smile and then the external world will smile back. It cannot happen any other way. It is impossible. It will not happen any other way. It is impossible, because "what you put out is what you get back" and this never changes.

Jefferson: Wow, Arvantis, good stuff!

Arvantis: We find it to be very effective in creating our world. Many other worlds that we interact with function this way too. As a result, we and those other worlds are filled with joy and abundance in uplifting ways. We are free from the darkness, in every sense, that your world experiences. But again, we understand your world has chosen to play in this game of darkness or limitation and separation, so we are in no way suggesting there is anything wrong with that.

Jefferson: What is the best way, Arvantis, to get our political process to move forward in positive directions on this planet? Will it achieve greater progress by first searching for the "kingdom of God," or do you have a suggestion?

Arvantis: Again, the kingdom of God is within. In realizing that, then you do not need to search. When people acknowledge it is within them, the search is over. And that then allows them to become more connected to the idea that they create their reality and to find the joy within them. By following their heart, they will begin finding inspirations to do certain things that will be exciting for them and some such people will be most excited to move into what you would consider your political arena. They will move into the governmental functions. This will occur in one country after the next. And they will carry forth their inner understanding that the kingdom of heaven is within. They will be able to share this reality in political vocabulary, in governmental vocabulary, so that other people already in governmental jobs will listen to them, and acknowledge them, and begin to get in touch with their own hearts more readily. They too will become more in tune to who they are by taking steps to let go of the old ideas and old ways.

So again, it comes down to following the heart! There will be some who will be inclined to move into political and governmental arenas in uplifting and joyful ways simply by following their heart. You have many people in your current governmental and political arenas that are there not from following their heart but for other reasons.

The change will occur in all of your society's infrastructure. As more people simply follow their heart, there will be more people excited to go into this arena or into that arena, into medicine, into religion, into education, into politics, into manufacturing, or into financial fields. Gradually their new consciousness will begin to be a catalyst that awakens other people already in those fields. Others will then become more open to recognize they are the Creator and the kingdom is within. They will begin to learn how to follow their heart and how to let go of the old manipulative ways.

Jefferson: Many people on Earth have met extraterrestrials. Some of the ETs they meet are their counterparts that exist on another planet in another timeline...like you are for me. These people may or may not remember meeting ETs, but still feel anxiety or fear around the topic of ETs. What suggestion do you have then to deal with such anxiety or fear?

Arvantis: Well, again, it comes down to following the heart. Recognizing they are the Creators of their realities. They are infinite loving beings.

Jefferson: Okay.

Arvantis: When they are truly in that state, they have nothing to fear, for fear does not exist in your true state of being. It is not a reality. When they truly learn that and hold that vibration of understanding, then when they are interacting with others there will be no issue. They will be fear free. They will not be frightened by the idea of interacting with extraterrestrials.

Presently, most of you have many thoughts and belief systems based on ideas of limitation and separation, such as the belief your god or creator is separate from you. These are alien to your true state of being.

In a sense, many of you have several alien ideas that you have hidden within your psyches due to misguided teachings about your true nature. For example, when you are in contact with an extraterrestrial that knows who it is, knows its true connection with Source, knows it is a creator, knows it is part of the Creator, then the person begins to vibrationally connect to that ETs knowing through the process of sympathetic resonance. The person instantly begins having thoughts that it too is part of the Creator. Because this knowing contradicts the person's alien ideas that suddenly come out of hiding, this person becomes extremely frightened.

Your society has been taught to believe so many alien ideas. For example, the alien idea that it's a sin to think you are part of the Creator and that if you have such a thought then God might send you to hell for eternity.

Jefferson: Yeah.

Arvantis: Immense fear can arise in a person when they suddenly start thinking they are a whole, infinite, Creator within and of their self.

By accepting who you truly are, then there will not be any more of the alien ideas within you. Thus then, when a person comes into contact with an extraterrestrial, there will not be any inner alien beliefs coming to the surface that are frightening.

As Earth humans come into contact with the alien ideas within themselves, and heal these discordant beliefs, and then recognize their self to be a whole Creator of infinite power and joy, then your frequency as Earth humans can begin to match those of the extraterrestrial beings that are presently around your Earth supporting you. And then you will be able to resonate together joyfully. And then physical contact can be comfortable, peaceful, pleasant, joyful, revealing, and a powerful nurturing relationship can be renewed, be reconnected. It has been a long time since Earth humans were last aware of the warm relationship that exists with extraterrestrials.

Jefferson: Are there other ET societies that would find in me, or in people who have a similar curiosity about ETs, a gateway through which they would be able to get there message across?

Arvantis: Well, they do have ideas they do like to share, and there are those then on your world who are more willing to be of that resonance, that vibration.

Jefferson: Okay.

Arvantis: And if you choose to be of that vibration, then they can connect to you more easily, more readily. But then it is always a choice that you are making to make that connection with them and to then bring forth information that they are sharing. It is always a choice that you are making to be a part of that, or not to be a part of that. Does that answer the question?

Jefferson: Yes, thank you. Where are you located right now Arvantis?

Arvantis: I am on a world that is approximately eighteen light years from Earth.

Jefferson: Why did you choose to mention the distance first?

Arvantis: That was something we felt would be most revealing.

Jefferson: What does that reveal?

Arvantis: Something that in time will corroborate with, in a sense, other ideas we have shared before and will share again in the future. And then there will be enough information so you can, in a sense, connect the dots and have a more whole picture of our interaction with you in these channeling sessions.

Jefferson: And are you alone?

Arvantis: No, there are several here.

Jefferson: And are they Arkoreuns?

Arvantis: There are a few, yes!

Jefferson: Say hello to them for me!

Arvantis: They hear you saying hello!

Jefferson: All right, very good! Is it day or night there?

Arvantis: It is a region of sunrise in our locale.

Jefferson: Now, as far as the postcard, how's it going?

Arvantis: We are working on it. This could take time before it is something you receive in the way you are looking for it.

Jefferson: Sure. And in general, the amount of time it takes for something to manifest is the same amount of time that it takes for an individual to be in vibrational alignment with it?

Arvantis: You could say that.

Jefferson: So basically, if I have not received it yet, it is because I am not in perfect alignment with that reality where I already have it?

Arvantis: You can create that idea, yes.

Jefferson: Can we create any reality?

Arvantis: Yes.

Jefferson: But given the momentum things have today, as you read the energies, there are things that I cannot create given my level of consciousness?

Arvantis: There are things that are less likely, less probable.

Jefferson: When you say you can...okay...that means that it is probable?

Arvantis: Yes. It is possible but not as probable, not as likely, but possible.

Jefferson: Could you expand on what is possible and what is probable?

Arvantis: Everything is possible!

Jefferson: Oh okay. But not everything is probable because it depends on many factors?

Arvantis: Yes!

Jefferson: People are always blaming circumstances in their life as the cause of failures they experience —

Arvantis: Well, you have simply to recognize that you are the one that is creating everything you experience. And whatever it is that you are creating that you seem to think you don't like, you have to come into acceptance that you are creating that as well.

Jefferson: Yeah, but it seems way too easy when you say you just have to acknowledge it, because —

Arvantis: It really is quite simple.

Jefferson: But what about all of the conditioning people have from all the limitations they have been taught?

Arvantis: They are creating all of that too.

Jefferson: So are you saying that when they acknowledge creating the limitations, then that energy will just vanish?

Arvantis: If they make the acknowledgement one hundred percent then it will vanish one hundred percent. If they acknowledge in steps, bit by bit, then the adjustments will be made step by step, bit by bit.

Jefferson: So the level of their acknowledgement determines, in a sense, the degree of heat that can melt the ice of their impeding beliefs so they can see clearly?

Arvantis: The more they accept it, the more powerful they will get confirmation of it.

Jefferson: Are extraterrestrials sensitized to all of the hardship we go through?

Arvantis: We don't, in that way, feel the despair that you do.

Jefferson: Do you feel pity for us?

Arvantis: We do not pity your choice to create a world that is a perfect reflection of your choices of what to create. You are creating perfectly what you are choosing to create.

Jefferson: Sure, sure, sure!

Arvantis: We do not pity the process of a Creator experiencing what it chooses to create. And you give us the opportunity to experience an aspect of Creation as it is creating something that it claims it doesn't prefer but keeps doing it anyway. We find it rather fascinating that you would embark on such a misperception of your true nature.

Jefferson: Okay. So basically, we humans are mythmakers in the sense that we have had the opportunity to take Creation to places it has never been before?

Arvantis: You can create the idea that it has never been there before but Creation is in all places simultaneously, in a place in which there is no time at all. You could say Earth humans are experiencing things they have not experienced before. But the Universe, Existence itself, is all things simultaneously. There is no experience then that it has not and is not.

Jefferson: So you don't pity us because you know this is an adventure. It is adding to all that we are becoming here, and it is something very enriching that is happening here?

Arvantis: Yes! And we have great love for your society, and for each of you as individuals. We learn from the choices you make and how you create what may seem to you to be hardships. We also in times when you are open, and willing, and asking, we will bring forth information that can help you let go of those old ideas so that you can reconnect more to your whole, true state of being.

Jefferson: If we figure out how to apply the process of change using the power of our imagination, then the energy that holds holographic like constructs together in physical reality can be changed too. We can redefine our reality at will. But is it really that easy?

Arvantis: Yes.

Jefferson: It is that easy?

Arvantis: How hard is it to get the reflection in the mirror to smile?

Jefferson: It is easy!

Arvantis: It can be that easy to manifest in your physical world!

Jefferson: Wow!

Arvantis: You merely need to get in touch with all of the belief systems that are preventing you from getting in front of the mirror and smiling, so to speak.

Jefferson: Wow.

Arvantis: How many people stand in front of a mirror and smile? Solely for the sake of seeing themselves smile? I share with you the percentage is extremely small. So then, how many people are really willing to make choices and changes in their belief systems so they can then have a more positive, wise, intelligent, upliftingly abundant experience in physical life?

Jefferson: Okay. Wow.

Arvantis: Many people look in the mirror every day rather somberly.

Jefferson: Okay.

Arvantis: How many people really take the time to smile and to get back the reflection of their physical reality smiling back upon them?

Jefferson: How many?

Arvantis: The numbers are very small, but they are growing. The "age of awareness and self-realization" is expanding and growing. There are more people who are willing to smile and see their reflection smiling. They are making great changes in their belief systems so they can experience life with a greater sense of smiling happiness. They are willing to make changes to create a physical life, to manifest a physical world, within their daily experience that is more smilingly happy and financially abundant.

Jefferson: All right, fantastic! Arvantis, when is the first public and peaceful contact going to happen?

Arvantis: When it is appropriate and your world and our world are most in alignment energetically.

Jefferson: Okay. Knowing the future…has it already happened?

Arvantis: That is something that is simultaneous with this present as is the past. It all exists here.

Jefferson: I see. But because of the changes that can happen and steer the collective to choose parallel versions of reality, you can't say exactly when, or where, or who, correct? Because of the nature of change?

Arvantis: In terms of how you create the idea of time and future, there is always some variation and flexibility in terms of when certain events will transpire, when they will occur, when they will happen, when they will manifest.

Jefferson: I see.

Arvantis: It comes down to when they are sufficiently putting out that particular frequency, that belief, that emotion sufficiently, thus then it becomes the strongest vibration they are putting out and thus then becomes the reality they connect to and experience being manifested.

Jefferson: So it's not —

Arvantis: The reality already exists. It is simply up to them to put out that reality the strongest with their thoughts, their emotions, their actions, their attitudes, their behaviors. And when they put out that particular idea the strongest, they then tune in to that reality. It already exists but to them it will seem like time has transpired and a future date has suddenly been reached.

Jefferson: Okay. So it's not about looking for contact with extraterrestrials more than it is to be all that you can be here and now?

Arvantis: Follow your heart to the best of your ability in each moment! Then you will be of greatest service, be most productive, and make all the contacts and connections that will be most beneficial for All That Is, which includes you in your current physical embodiment on Earth. It is that simple.

Jefferson: Would you say the four Laws of Creation encompass everything, and if so, why would the 2012 quarantine — that asks ETs not to have public contact with us until a certain date — why would the 2012 quarantine even be necessary?

Arvantis: You have created a world, a play, in which you want to have certain rules and laws upheld.

Jefferson: Yes.

Arvantis: So it is like having certain sets in the play, certain structures for you to then have an experience within. And so there then must be a quarantine that, in a sense, excludes us from the set, from the stage of the current play your society as a collective has chosen to produce and to act within. It doesn't do any good to have a movie that is set in the 1950s if you have rockets, and jets, and sports cars zooming about in the streets.

Jefferson: Fantastic analogy!

Arvantis: You have created a play in which extraterrestrials don't suit the theme.

Jefferson: Okay. So wouldn't you say that the third Law of Creation, aka, the Law of Attraction, "what you put out is what you get back," wouldn't that be enough to keep extraterrestrials away?

Arvantis: How?

Jefferson: Oh, that is true, because we would at individual levels give off lower vibrations as we would be still evolving then we would bring to us lower vibrational beings.

Arvantis: We do not understand the question.

Jefferson: Okay. There is a quarantine in place. Aren't the four Laws of Creation sufficient enough?

Arvantis: How?

Jefferson: How? Like…with the Law of Attraction, we would not bring to us those ET beings that we are not wanting to interact with!

Arvantis: How does that prevent an extraterrestrial from coming to your world?

Jefferson: Because we are not giving off a vibration that is a match to extraterrestrials!

Arvantis: There are those who do give off an interest in extraterrestrials.

Jefferson: I see. Yeah, I understand now. As soon as I finished asking, I got my own answer, and that is exactly it. All right, Arvantis, any final message?

Arvantis: We thank you for sharing and embarking upon this journey with us in this collection of chapters and information to be shared in the book format. It is a great joy for us as a society to be able to interact with you, in a sense, as an ambassador of this information on your planet at this timing with us in our contact with you. We are appreciative of your choices, and we are most grateful!

We look forward to interactions with you again in the future. We understand your society is going through many changes at this time. We realize it is something that will take time before we are fully accepted in your society's aware conscious state of being sufficiently so that we can then meet with you physically, heart to heart, eye to eye, and share and enrich one another in that way as well.

Before contact does occur, there is much more your society has to explore within itself, much more your society has in terms of experiences that will unfold in your world's day to day living that can be greatly exciting for most of you, wonderfully nourishing and enriching for your society as a whole as well.

All of these exciting experiences would be missed by you if we were already with you there today. So it is important that you continue to follow your heart and not get stuck on the idea that you just want to have us on Earth right now. There are many experiences of great joy yet to unfold for your society without extraterrestrials being present on your world. So be open to the exciting experiences that can take place in a world that still believes it is the only human life-form in existence.

Allow for more people to come into those moments of excitement when they realize who they truly are. Give more people time as individuals to wake up, for the light bulb of their heart center desires to go off and illuminate and awaken within their sensorial, joyful state of being, that can bring tears of joy strolling and streaming down their soft facial contours. Allow for more individuals to have this wonderful realizational experience to occur within their life.

In time, as more people have this awakening, there will become a strong enough vibration on your planet to hold connection with our society and other extraterrestrial societies so we can have open, peaceful contact with you on your planet face to face, heart to heart.

There is great joy in our society for human beings on Earth! We love your society and individuals, all as a whole and each as an individual, without exception. And we thank you for having chosen to share with us in this way. We look forward, again as we have said, to more such meetings in your future as you create the idea of future to exist!

Jefferson: A fascinating journey to you and to your society too! On behalf of those who will agree with me, within and as this human race and sure enough will enjoy this idea: I intend that every time a human being finishes reading this book — whether they believe this to be possible or not — that a rainbow of gratitude becomes visible to your civilization as a token of our most enlightening exchange and appreciation for your willingness to assist and support us with respect, trust, infinite patience, and unconditional love!

And this is what I most want your society to hear in their hearts when they see the rainbows, "Ahr in tor kai mor ren!"

Arvantis: Ahr in tor kai mor ren! Ahr in tor kai mor ren! Yes! Thank you. Much joy and love to you dear one! Until we meet again, most wonderfully delicious good day to you!

Jefferson: Thank you indeed! See you!

"Ahr in tor kai mor ren"
- Arvantis

Translation:
"There is much love in our hearts for all of you."

About the Authors

Shaun Swanson

Shaun is an author, a teacher, and a channel for members of our human extraterrestrial family including Ishuwa of the Yahyel, Arvantis of the Arkoreuns, and Onkor of the Sassani. Shaun has appeared on television and radio programs. He graduated with a Bachelor of Arts degree in Business Economics from the University of California at Santa Barbara, UCSB.

Since 1996, Shaun has been doing channeling consultations as a form of counseling and healing for people pursuing spiritual growth, self empowerment, personal transformation, and self realization.

In his "Sounds of Light" workshops, he teaches on topics that include: "The Reality Creation Process," "The Nature and Structure of Our Infinitely Supportive Youniverse," "The Four Laws of Creation," and "How To Always Create In Harmony With Your Heart's Infinite Ecstasies!"

Shaun is co-author of the book "Avatars of the Phoenix Lights UFO: Ishuwa and the Yahyel."

For more information about Shaun's public channeling events and private channeling consultations with Ishuwa, visit {www.Ishuwa.com} and {www. youtube.com/ user/ ishuwadotcom}.

Jefferson Viscardi

Jefferson Viscardi has a Ph.D. degree, Philosopher of Metaphysical Life Coaching, from the University of Metaphysical Sciences distance learning facility. He is certified by the International Association of Reiki Professionals as a Reiki healer, level III, in the Usui System of natural healing. He teaches on topics such as: extraterrestrials, our galactic family, and Christ consciousness.

Jefferson is a co-author of "Avatars of the Phoenix Lights UFO: Ishuwa and the Yahyel," and "The Circle of Light and The Philosopher." He is the author of "Insights with Adronis from Sirius." He also wrote "Construindo uma Sociedade Iluminada" in Portuguese. More info at {www.JeffersonViscardi.com}.

Arvantis

Arvantis is a feline human. He resides in a different solar system and is part of our intergalactic family. He is an interstellar explorer and a biologist. His society is called the Arkoreuns. He comes to us from what we call our future. Many Earth humans are genetically connected to the Arkoreuns. To learn more about Arvantis and his civilization, visit {www. youtube.com/user/felinehumanoid}
and {www.Arvantis.org}

8438314R1

Made in the USA
Charleston, SC
09 June 2011